T0311816

Cambridge Elements ☰

Elements in the Philosophy of Ludwig Wittgenstein
edited by
David G. Stern
University of Iowa

WITTGENSTEIN ON SENSE AND GRAMMAR

Silver Bronzo
National Research University Higher School of Economics, Moscow

CAMBRIDGE
UNIVERSITY PRESS

CAMBRIDGE
UNIVERSITY PRESS

University Printing House, Cambridge CB2 8BS, United Kingdom

One Liberty Plaza, 20th Floor, New York, NY 10006, USA

477 Williamstown Road, Port Melbourne, VIC 3207, Australia

314–321, 3rd Floor, Plot 3, Splendor Forum, Jasola District Centre,
New Delhi – 110025, India

103 Penang Road, #05–06/07, Visioncrest Commercial, Singapore 238467

Cambridge University Press is part of the University of Cambridge.

It furthers the University's mission by disseminating knowledge in the pursuit of
education, learning, and research at the highest international levels of excellence.

www.cambridge.org
Information on this title: www.cambridge.org/9781108977395
DOI: 10.1017/9781108973359

First published 2022

A catalogue record for this publication is available from the British Library.

ISBN 978-1-108-97739-5 Paperback
ISSN 2632-7112 (online)
ISSN 2632-7104 (print)

Wittgenstein on Sense and Grammar

Elements in the Philosophy of Ludwig Wittgenstein

DOI: 10.1017/9781108973359
First published online: May 2022

Silver Bronzo
National Research University Higher School of Economics, Moscow

Author for correspondence: Silver Bronzo, silver.bronzo@gmail.com

Abstract: The distinction between sense and nonsense is central to Wittgenstein's philosophy. It is at the basis of his conception of philosophy as a struggle against illusions of sense generated by misunderstandings of the logic of our language. Moreover, it informs the notions of "grammar" (in the later work) and "logical syntax" (in the early work), whose investigation serves to clear up those misunderstandings. This Element contrasts two exegetical approaches: one grounding charges of nonsensicality in a theory of sense specifying criteria that are external to the linguistic performance under indictment; and one rejecting any such theory. The former pursues the idea of a nonsensicality test; the latter holds that illusions of sense can only be overcome from within, through the very capacity of which they constitute defective exercises. The Element connects the two approaches to opposite understandings of Wittgenstein's conception of language, and defends a version of the second approach.

Keywords: nonsense, logical syntax, grammar, philosophy, clarification

ISBNs: 9781108977395 (PB), 9781108973359 (OC)
ISSNs: 2632-7112 (online), 2632-7104 (print)

Contents

1 Introduction

1.1 Delimiting the Topic

This Element deals with Wittgenstein's conception of the contrast between saying something that makes sense and failing to do so or falling into nonsense.* When one succeeds in saying something that makes sense – as the phrase will be used in this Element – one correctly takes oneself, and indeed knows, to be doing so. Conversely, when one falls into nonsense, one does not know it. On the contrary, one tries to say something that makes sense and mistakenly takes oneself to be doing so: one undergoes an illusion of sense. In short, this Element is concerned with saying something that makes sense as a *fallible self-conscious capacity*.[1]

Not all nonsense is something that one *falls into*. There are ways of employing the terms "nonsense" and "nonsensical sentence" that do not correspond to the idea of failing to say something that makes sense. Wittgenstein sometimes uses the terms in these other ways. He speaks, for example, of the babbling of a child or a nonsense poem as forms of nonsense (PI §282). Clearly, these linguistic or protolinguistic phenomena do not express failures to say something that makes sense. The infant who is just starting to babble has no conception of what it is to speak meaningfully; hence, they are not trying, but failing, to do so. They are still acquiring the capacity to speak meaningfully, not failing to exercise it successfully. The author of a nonsense poem is also not failing to say something to make sense, even though for very different reasons. They, clearly, have acquired the capacity to speak meaningfully, but are not failing to exercise it successfully, because they are not even trying to do so. Their goal is not to say something that makes sense, even though it depends in complex ways on that capacity. While Wittgenstein occasionally employs the term "nonsense" in these and other similar ways, the notion of nonsense that figures most prominently – and arguably, also most fundamentally – in his writings is nonsense as the expression of a failure to say something that makes sense. This is the notion with which this Element is primarily concerned.

Just as one may or may not succeed in *saying* something that makes sense, one may or may not succeed in *thinking* something that makes sense without saying anything. While Wittgenstein does not deny that we can think without speaking, his primary object of investigation is spoken thought, or thinking *in*

---

* I wish to thank David Stern, Wim Vanrie and two anonymous referees for detailed comments that led to substantial improvements of this text.

[1] A capacity to Φ is "self-conscious," in the sense here relevant, if when one Φ-s, one thereby knows to be Φ-ing – and when one fails to Φ, one thereby fails to know to be failing to Φ, but mistakenly takes oneself to be Φ-ing. Section 1.7 comments on the choice of framing the issue in terms of "capacities," which is not a characteristically Wittgensteinian term.

speaking. This is for him the key for understanding thought in general. For this reason, he is often listed as one of the main representatives of the "linguistic turn" in twentieth-century philosophy. What sort of priority, exactly, Wittgenstein attributes to spoken over unspoken thought, and whether his view on the matter changed over the course of his career, are debatable questions. One may hold, for instance, that early Wittgenstein adopted a comparatively weak version of the linguistic turn, according to which spoken and unspoken thought have essentially the same nature and the former has merely heuristic priority, whereas the later Wittgenstein adopted a stronger version of the linguistic turn, according to which spoken thought constitutes the conceptually fundamental form of thinking. In any case, the main concern of this Element is making sense construed as a *linguistic* achievement.

The rest of this Introduction will give an overview of how the contrast between sense and nonsense is connected to Wittgenstein's conception of philosophy on the one hand, and to his conception of logical syntax and grammar on the other. The subsequent sections will contrast two approaches to these regions of Wittgenstein's thought. The Element as a whole focuses on points of continuity in Wittgenstein's philosophy. Discontinuities will be mentioned only when this serves to bring out the underlying continuities.

1.2 Sense, Nonsense, and Philosophy

The contrast between sense and nonsense is at the basis of one of the most distinctive and controversial aspects of Wittgenstein's thought, namely his conception of philosophy. For Wittgenstein, philosophical problems are not well-posed questions that admit of intelligible answers, as happens paradigmatically with questions of natural science. On the contrary, philosophical questions and their purported answers are nonsensical. Philosophy as Wittgenstein seeks to practice it aims to expose their nonsensicality. As Wittgenstein puts it in the *Tractatus Logico-Philosophicus*: "Most propositions and questions, that have been written about philosophical matters, are not false, but nonsensical. We cannot, therefore, answer questions of this kind at all, but only state their nonsensicality" (TLP 4.003). The same perspective appears in his major later work, the *Philosophical Investigations*: "My aim is: to teach you to pass from a piece of disguised nonsense to something that is patent nonsense" (PI §464); "The results of philosophy are the uncovering of one or another piece of plain nonsense" (PI §119). Philosophical problems, along with their purported positive solutions, only appear to make sense. They generate illusions of sense, and the goal of philosophy is to make us aware of such illusions, in a progress from disguised to overt nonsense. For Wittgenstein, we can say, the object of philosophy is our capacity to make sense. Philosophy seeks to identify its failures and, in this manner, to confer on us a firmer grasp of the capacity.

The illusions of sense that philosophy seeks to dissolve derive, for Wittgenstein, from a certain sort of misunderstanding – one concerning the use of words figuring in the formulation of philosophical problems. Wittgenstein often refers to it as a "misunderstanding of the logic of our language." The problem is that we are prone to form a wrong conception of the use of linguistic expressions, and in particular, to assimilate the use of some expressions to the use of other expressions that work in fact very differently. In the preface to the *Tractatus*, he writes: "The book deals with the problems of philosophy and shows, as I believe, that the method of formulating these problems rests on the misunderstanding of the logic of our language" (TLP, preface; see also TLP 4.003). Later on in the same book, he traces this sort of misunderstanding to the misleading analogies of ordinary language – specifically, to the fact that the same linguistic expression is often used in different ways (for instance, the word "is" is used sometimes as the copula and sometimes as the sign of identity, as in "Socrates is wise" and "Socrates is the teacher of Plato" respectively), and to the fact that linguistic expressions which function differently can often appear to be used in the same way (for instance, the verbs "to go" and "to exist" can appear, qua intransitive verbs, to function similarly in "Cars go" and "Cars exist"; TLP 3.323–3.3324). A version of the same idea is restated in the *Investigations*, even though in this later work Wittgenstein maintains that misleading linguistic analogies are only *one* of the causes of the misunderstanding of the use of linguistic expressions: "Our investigation … sheds light on our problem by clearing misunderstandings away. Misunderstandings concerning the use of words, caused, among other things, by certain analogies between the forms of expression in different regions of language" (PI §90). In other passages, he employs the same terminology that he used in the *Tractatus*, speaking of a "misunderstanding of the logic of language" (PI §93) and of the "temptation to misunderstand the logic of our expressions" (PI §345).

If the goal of philosophy is to unmask failures to make sense caused by misunderstandings of the use of linguistic expressions, it is to be expected that philosophy, in order to achieve its goal, will have to clear up those misunderstandings – that is, to clarify how linguistic expressions are used. This is in fact Wittgenstein's view, both early and late. Philosophy as he seeks to practice it is an activity of clarification of the use of linguistic expressions.

1.3 Clarification and Grammar

In the *Investigations*, Wittgenstein calls the sort of inquiry that seeks to clarify the use of linguistic expressions "grammatical" (PI §90). He uses the term "grammar" and its cognates to characterize both the inquiry and its object, namely the "grammar" of linguistic expressions (as in, "the grammar of 'to mean' is not like that of the expression 'to imagine,'" PI §38). The grammar of linguistic expressions is also referred to as their "logic" (as in, "we are under a temptation to misunderstand the logic of our expressions," PI §345) and their "use" (as in, "Grammar ... only describes ... the use of signs," PI §496).

It is important for the *Investigations* that a grammatical inquiry can take different forms: there is more than one way of clarifying the use of words, whose effectiveness depends on the misunderstanding at issue. This accords with the book's explicit methodological pluralism: "There is not *a* philosophical method, though there are indeed methods, like different therapies" (PI §133). Everything in the *Investigations* suggests that there is no closed list of such methods: one has to look and see what works in each particular case. Thus, one way of clarifying the use of linguistic expressions is "analysis," construed as the process of "substituting one form of expression for another" (PI §90); another is "finding and inventing intermediate cases" between different uses of words (PI §122); another is asking "how a proposition can be verified" (PI §353); another is describing "clear and simple language-games" that should throw light on the use of our language by serving as "objects of comparison" (PI §130); another is attending to how the meaning of a word is taught or explained (see, for example, PI §9, even though this is a pervasive procedure of the *Investigations*); another is bringing ourselves to find remarkable the use of some expression that we initially take to be unproblematic, in order to come to see as unproblematic the use of some other expression that we initially find puzzling (PI §524); and yet another method consists in giving what Wittgenstein calls – in equivalent or closely related ways – "grammatical propositions" (PI §§251, 295, 458), "grammatical notes" (PI §232), "grammatical remarks" (PI §574), and "grammatical rules" (PI §497). These are sentences that describe the use of linguistic expressions. Sentences that are explicitly characterized in this way in the *Investigations* include: "Every rod has a length" (PI §252); "An order orders its own execution" (PI §458); "A sentence, and hence in another sense a thought, can be the 'expression' of belief, hope, expectation, etc. But believing is not thinking" (PI §574); "I can know what someone else is thinking, not what I am thinking. It is correct to say 'I know what you are thinking', and wrong to say 'I know what I am thinking'" (PI, II, xi, p. 222).

Wittgenstein insists that grammar "only describes" the use of signs (PI §496; see also §124). Yet, as the terms "grammar" and "grammatical rule" suggest, this is a sort of description that involves a normative dimension. The description of the use of linguistic expressions that Wittgenstein recommends does not consist in empirical generalizations about how a given population of speakers uses given expressions. Such generalizations would have to treat *indifferently* the "good" and the "bad" cases, namely the cases where one succeeds in using an expression to make sense, and those in which one mistakenly takes oneself to be doing so. However, it is unclear how such generalizations could help to expose the bad cases as such. In fact, one of Wittgenstein's negative character-izations of a grammatical inquiry is that it is *not* empirical (PI §251, for example, contrasts grammatical propositions with empirical propositions). Wittgensteinian grammar seeks to describe how words are used *to make sense*. We can also say: they seek to describe the *successful exercise* of the capacity to use words to make sense. After all, Wittgenstein holds that we need to get a clear view of the "functioning" of words (PI §5) and of the "workings" of language (PI §109) – not of their *mal*functioning and *mis*workings.[2]

The *Tractatus* does not say that it pursues a "grammatical inquiry" consisting, among other things, in giving "grammatical propositions" or stating "grammat-ical rules." But the *Tractatus*, too, seeks to clarify how linguistic expressions are used to make sense. Philosophy, it says, is an "activity" whose result is "the clarification of propositions" (TLP 4.112). Just as the *Investigations* holds that "Philosophy is a battle against the bewitchment of our intelligence by means of language" (PI §109), so the *Tractatus* states that "All philosophy is critique of language" (TLP 4.0031). The *Tractatus*, like the *Investigations*, seeks to remove misunderstandings about the functioning of language and dissolve in this way the ensuing philosophical problems. For instance, and proceeding roughly from the beginning to the end of the book, the *Tractatus* seeks to show that "senseful propositions" (*Sinnvolle Sätze*), stating truly or falsely how things stand, func-tion differently from names, picking out something we want to talk about;[3] that the so-called truth-predicate ("is true") and analogous expressions ("is a fact," "obtains," "is the case") function differently from genuine predicates ascribing a property to some kind of entity (such as "is wise"); that truth-functional connectives ("if," "and," etc.) function differently from genuine predicates; that numerals function differently from names; that propositional attitude reports (such as "S judges/says p") function differently from relational proposi-tions (such as "A loves B"); that senseful propositions function differently – and in each case in a different way – from identity statements, the so-called propositions of logic (such as the law of noncontradiction), mathematical equations, probability statements, the fundamental laws of physics, the so-called propositions of ethics, and the so-called propositions with which

---

[2] This does not deny that, for Wittgenstein, the ultimate goal of describing the functioning of language is to identify cases in which it malfunctions.

[3] A Tractarian *Satz* is a linguistic entity. A less common but perhaps clearer translation is "sentence" rather than "proposition."

a work of philosophy such as the *Tractatus* seeks to clarify the functioning of language. In each case, the *Tractatus* opposes a false assimilation of uses of language.[4]

1.4 Grammatical Remarks and Tractarian Elucidations

While the *Tractatus* and the *Investigations* are alike in pursuing the clarification of the use of language, they differ in various ways about how to pursue this clarificatory work. One major difference concerns their respective views about the status of clarificatory language.

There is a question about how to conceive the functioning of the sentences that serve to clarify the functioning of language. One of the fundamental misunderstandings of the logic of our language that Wittgenstein addresses arises precisely with regard to this use of language. In particular, Wittgenstein thinks that it is a common mistake to construe this use of language on the model of contingent, empirical statements, belonging to what Wittgenstein sometimes calls "natural science." The traditional characterization of philosophy as the study of "necessary and apriori truths" is an expression of this sort of misunderstanding in so far as it takes the notion of truth that applies to empirical claims and then seeks to capture what is specific to philosophy by adding some external qualification. The well-known pronouncement that philosophy is not a "theory" (TLP 4.112, PI §109), which tends to alienate many of Wittgenstein's readers or would-be readers, must be understood and assessed in the context of these preoccupations about, we might say, the logic of philosophical language: not only the language that occurs in the formulation of alleged philosophical problems and their purported direct solutions, but also the language that is used to show that those alleged problems rest on misunderstandings of the use of linguistic expressions.

For the *Tractatus*, the sentences that seek to clarify the use of language achieve their purpose only in so far as they are eventually recognized as nonsensical. The *Tractatus* says that "a philosophical work consists essentially of elucidations" (TLP 4.112) and presents itself as such a work. In the penultimate numbered remark of the book, Wittgenstein writes: "My sentences elucidate in this way: he who understands me finally recognizes them as nonsensical, when he has climbed out through them, on them, over them. (He must so to speak throw away the ladder, after he has climbed up on it.)" (TLP 6.54). So, the ultimate goal of philosophy is to help us become aware of illusions of sense; it

---

[4] For a discussion of the Tractarian recognition of various uses of language besides the fact-stating or "picturing" use (which is laid out by the so-called "picture theory of the proposition"), see Kremer (2002) and Diamond (2011, 2019).

does so by clarifying the use of linguistic expressions; and it does *this* – namely, clarifying the use of linguistic expressions – by giving us sentences that fulfil their function only in so far as they are initially taken to make sense (and arguably, to make sense in the specific way in which Tractarian *sinnvolle Sätze* make sense), but are eventually seen to express mere illusions of sense. More briefly: in order to help us overcome failures to make sense, philosophy should first lead us into *more* failures to make sense and then make us recognize those failures as such.

There is a question about whether this procedure is inherently paradoxical, but in any case, there is no commitment to it in the *Investigations*. This later book contains nothing analogous to TLP 6.54. It does not state that its method for clarifying the functioning of language is the employment of sentences that must be eventually recognized as nonsensical. In particular, there is no sugges- tion that "grammatical remarks" are supposed to function in this way. One way of understanding this difference is that the *Tractatus*' method of elucidations and the *Investigations*' method of grammatical remarks are mutually compat- ible and could in principle be used in tandem. On this reading, the *Investigations* could in principle admit the *Tractarian* elucidatory method in its pantheon of clarificatory tools, and the *Tractatus* (in so far as it holds that a work of philosophy consists "essentially," but not exclusively, of elucidations) could in principle admit the use of grammatical remarks as a subsidiary clarificatory device. Another way of understanding the matter is that the two methods are mutually incompatible, because they express alternative views about the *same* sort of undertaking. On this other reading, there is no room in the *Tractatus* for grammatical remarks, and no room in the *Investigations* for a Tractarian eluci- dation. What the *Investigations* regards as a grammatical remark would have to be conceived for the *Tractatus* as an elucidation, and what the *Tractatus* regards as an elucidation would have to be conceived for the *Investigations* as a grammatical remark.[5]

Whether or not Tractarian elucidations and grammatical remarks are mutu- ally compatible, they are supposed to function very differently. A Tractarian elucidation is construed as an *essentially transitional* use of language: it achieves its purpose only if it is first taken to make sense and then recognized as nonsensical. The *Investigations* provides different positive characterizations of what goes on in a grammatical remark. A first feature of grammatical remarks is that they purport to "remind" us of something we already know: "The work of the philosopher consists in assembling reminders for a particular purpose" (PI

---

[5] The relation between Tractarian elucidations and grammatical remarks is a debated topic. See, for instance, McGinn (2006) and Moyal-Sharrock (2007).

§127). Also, "The problems are solved, not by giving new information, but by arranging what we have always known" (PI §109; see also PI §89). A second feature of grammatical remarks is that they do not purport to put forth anything controversial: "If one tried to advance *theses* in philosophy, it would never be possible to debate them, because everybody would agree to them" (PI §128). A third feature of grammatical remarks is that they get their purpose – that is, their *whole* purpose – from the philosophical problems they serve to dissolve: "We must do away with all *explanation*, and description alone must take its place. And this description gets its light, that is to say its purpose, from the philosophical problems" (PI §109).

Arguably, this is only an entry of a much longer list of differences between Wittgenstein's early and later conception of clarification. However, the background of these differences is a general agreement about the ultimate goal of philosophy – namely, dissolving philosophical problems by clarifying the functioning of language – and the necessity to resist the assimilation of clarificatory uses of language to the statement of contingent, empirical facts.

1.5 Grammar and Syntax

While the *Tractatus* does not purport to give grammatical remarks, it does mention "logical grammar" as a synonym of "logical syntax" (TLP 3.325). It also speaks of the "logicosyntactical employment" of linguistic expressions (TLP 3.327) and of "rules of logical syntax" (TLP 3.334, 3.344). A precursor of this terminology appears in the 1914 *Notes Dictated to Moore*, where Wittgenstein equates "rules of logic" with "syntactical rules for the manipulation of symbols" (NB 117). After his return to full-time philosophy in 1929, he continued for a few years to speak of "syntactical rules" (see, for example, RLF 162, PR §78, BT 206/264) and of the "syntax" of linguistic expressions (BT 429/636). He also began to speak of "propositions of syntax" (PR §§132, 177, BT 212/270). In this period, Wittgenstein appears to use "syntax" and "grammar" interchangeably. For instance, in a lecture delivered in 1933, he reportedly said, "Just as 'sense' is vague, so must be 'grammar,' 'grammatical rule,' 'syntax'" (MWL 282). The grammar talk however becomes increasingly more frequent, and in the *Blue and Brown Books* (BB), dictated between 1933 and 1935, there is no trace left of the syntax talk. The same applies to the *Investigations*.

There are certainly important differences between the "logical syntax" of the *Tractatus* and the "grammar" of the *Investigations*. However, at a sufficiently high level of abstraction, they are equivalent: like grammar, logical syntax describes how linguistic expressions are used *to make sense* – and thus the functioning of language, as opposed to its malfunctioning. In a different registry of the terminology, just as the grammar of an expression is its meaningful use (as opposed to its nonsensical, and thus defective, application), so is its logical syntax.

The connection between Tractarian logical syntax and sense is particularly explicit in a passage written in 1929, when Wittgenstein's views were still in many respects very close to the *Tractatus*. The paragraph begins with a paraphrase of the sections of the *Tractatus* that introduce the topic leading to the discussion of logical syntax (TLP 3.31–3.315), and then continues: "By syntax . . . I mean the rules which tell us in which connections only a word gives sense, thus excluding nonsensical structures" (RLF 162). The connection is almost as explicit in a letter that Wittgenstein wrote before the first bilingual publication of the *Tractatus* in 1922. The letter was addressed to one of his English translators, and the relevant passage discusses the translation of TLP 3.325, which was eventually rendered as: "In order to recognize the symbol in the sign we must consider the significant use [*sinnvolle Gebrauch*]." In his comments, Wittgenstein equates, first, "how [the] sign is *used* significantly in propositions" with "how the sign is used in accordance with the laws of logical syntax," and secondly, "significant use" with "syntactically correct use" (LO 59). Most plausibly, this means that the *syntactically correct* use of a sign is intended to contrast with a *nonsensical* combination of signs.[6]

The *Tractatus* introduces the terminology of "logical syntax" in a context that deals explicitly with the use of language that pertains to senseful propositions (*sinnvolle Sätze*), which state truly or falsely contingent states of affairs. Arguably, this is for the *Tractatus* the central use of language, in the sense that all other uses occupy a derivative position. It is thus reasonable to maintain that logical syntax, in the strict Tractarian understanding of the term, deals with the use of signs to "make sense" in a restricted understanding of the phrase – namely, to express a Tractarian "sense" (*Sinn*), which amounts to stating a contingent state of affairs. However, as the *Tractatus* acknowledges a variety of other uses of language (Section 1.3), it would not go against the spirit of the book to speak of logical syntax in an extended sense of the expression, so that the "logicosyntactical employment" of signs is in general *any* intelligible use of signs, as opposed to a way of mobilizing signs that results in nonsense. The contrast between "syntactically correct" and "syntactically incorrect" uses of signs, so understood, is a contrast between all the cases in which language is at work, fulfilling an intelligible function, and those in which

---

[6] For a different reading of the passage, see Johnston (2007), who takes the "syntactically correct use" to contrast with a semantically contentful use.

it fails to do so – running idle, or going on holiday, as Wittgenstein would later put it (PI §38). On this capacious construal of the terminology, one can say that the *Tractatus* addresses problems that rest on a misunderstanding of the logical syntax of our language, and that Tractarian elucidations seek to clarify the logical syntax of language.

1.6 Grammar, Form, and Content

Whenever words are not synonymous, they have in an obvious sense a different use. For instance, "Socrates" and "Plato," as names of different philosophers, have a different use. We saw above (Section 1.3) that Wittgenstein tends to speak equivalently of the "use" and the "grammar" of linguistic expressions. This equivalence, joined with the obvious sense of "use" just mentioned, entails that "Socrates" and "Plato" have a different grammar.

However, this is *not* the sort of difference that Wittgenstein is typically concerned with when he investigates the "grammar" of an expression. Take for instance the claim, in the *Investigations*, that "the grammar of 'to mean' is not like that of the expression 'to imagine'" (PI §38). Or take this other remark: "One might say 'Thinking is an incorporeal process' . . . if one were using this to distinguish the grammar of the word 'think' from that of, say, the word 'eat'" (PI §339). If the point here were simply that "to mean" and "to imagine," or "to think" and "to eat," have different meanings, it is hard to see how it would be worth making. Moreover, it is hard to see how pointing out mere differences in meaning could help to remove the sort of misunderstanding that Wittgenstein is interested in, namely misunderstandings leading to illusions of sense. It can indeed remove misunderstandings to point out, for example, that "Moscow" is the name of a city in Russia but also a city in Idaho. If I tell a friend that I am moving to Moscow, they might form the false belief that I am moving to Russia while I am in fact moving to Idaho, and they might ask questions that they would not ask if they had correctly understood what I wanted to say. However, this is simply a case of miscommunication (taking a certain form of words to mean X when in fact they mean Y), whereas Wittgenstein is interested in cases that give rise to an illusion of sense (taking a certain form of words to mean something when in fact they mean nothing at all).

We may distinguish, within the overall "use" or "grammar" of a word, its *content* and its *grammatical* (or *logical*) *form*. Wittgenstein is generally interested in the latter, and when he argues that two expressions have a different grammar, he generally aims to establish that they do not merely differ in content, but also in grammatical form. The distinction is here to be understood along the following lines. Two expressions may have different contents but the same grammatical form. This plausibly applies to "Socrates" and "Plato," or "Moscow" (Idaho) and "Moscow" (Russia). Two expressions have the same grammatical form if and only if they have the same *kind* of content, where the relevant kind is individuated by relations of substitutability *salva significatione*. In other words, two expressions have the same grammatical form if and only if they can be substituted for one another in all the contexts in which they are meaningfully employed without generating nonsense, under the assumption that one does not impart a new understanding on the substituted expression or on relevant features of the context in which it is embedded. Take, for example, the statement "Socrates died drinking hemlock." If we substitute "Plato" for "Socrates," we certainly say something different, turning the initial true statement into a false one; but the new statement, in spite of its falsity, makes sense. By contrast, suppose that we want to replace "Socrates" in our original statement with "yellow," as this is used in "Gold is yellow," obtaining "Yellow died drinking hemlock." Here the new sentence does not make any obvious sense, unless we understand "yellow" or "died drinking hemlock" in some different and less obvious way. If correct, this shows that "Socrates" as it occurs in "Socrates dies drinking hemlock," and "yellow" as it occurs in "Gold is yellow," have different grammatical forms.

A distinction of this sort between form and content is well-engrained in the philosophical tradition and a version of it appears in the *Tractatus* (TLP 3.31). Another traditional notion that Wittgenstein employs for similar purposes is that of a *category*. He writes, for instance: "'Infinite class' and 'finite class' are different logical categories; what can be meaningfully asserted of the one category cannot be meaningfully asserted of the other" (BT 492/745; see also BT 355/501 for a similar use of the expression "grammatical category"). A category, as opposed to a mere kind of thing, is defined by its connection to meaningfulness. Red apples and green apples are different kinds of things, but belong to the same category, in so far as anything that can be meaningfully said of the former can be meaningfully said of the latter and vice versa. Using this terminology, we can say that Wittgenstein's interest in the grammar of a linguistic expression is generally an interest in its grammatical category. It is a misunderstanding of this aspect of the use of a linguistic expression – as opposed to a mere misunderstanding of its content – that can intelligibly lead to illusions of sense. By mistakenly assimilating the grammatical forms or categories of two expressions, we can come to wrongly believe that we may meaningfully employ one expression in all the contexts in which we employ the other. For instance, by assimilating the grammatical category of "infinite class" to that of "finite class," we can think that we may ask of an infinite class the same questions that we may ask of a finite class.

Determining what counts as mere content as opposed to form or category in particular cases may be far from trivial. In fact, it would not be an exaggeration to say that the difficulty of this determination is the same as the difficulty of philosophical clarification as Wittgenstein conceives it. His philosophy, both early and late, can be seen as a sustained attempt to show that what we tend to conceive as mere differences in content are in fact differences in form or category.

These considerations must be reconciled with the fact that Wittgenstein frequently employs the terms "use" and "grammar" to include the content as well as the form or category of an expression. In the *Investigations* he famously states: "For a *large* class of cases – though not for all – in which we employ the word 'meaning' it can be defined thus: the meaning of a word is its use in the language" (PI §43). While there are senses of "meaning" that Wittgenstein does not equate with use (including, possibly, the employment of the term to desig-nate the feelings associated with a word), it is clear from the context of the remark that the sense in which "Socrates" and "Plato" have different meanings (because they name different persons) is intended to fall within the scope of the equation. So mere differences in content are regarded in that passage as differ-ences in use. Similarly, in the *Big Typescript*, Wittgenstein characterizes "mean-ing" as "the location of a word in grammar" (BT 26/31), maintains that "[t]o teach the meaning of a word means teaching its use" (BT 27/31), and argues that an ostensive definition, fixing the meaning of a word, "belongs to grammar" (BT 38/42 v). It is clear that, in these passages, the scope of grammar is not limited to form.

There are various points that Wittgenstein wants to make by including in the grammar of an expression its content as well as its grammatical form. In the chapters of the *Big Typescript* containing the previous passages, the main point is that fixing the content of a word – and thus connecting language to reality – is always done *in* language. This is true, the *Big Typescript* argues, also for ostensive definition, even though it employs nonverbal language. The idea that ostensive definition allows us to get outside language altogether and occupy a sideways-on perspective on language and reality from which the former can be connected to the latter is just an illusion. Saying that ostensive definition belongs to grammar is a way of expressing this point. This illustrates the fact that Wittgenstein has good reasons for employing a comprehensive notion of grammar or use that is sensitive to mere differences in content. Yet the existence of these motivations is fully compatible with the fact that the sort of misunder-standing that Wittgenstein seeks to dispel – and consequently, the sort of grammatical inquiry he pursues – concerns the *grammatical form* of linguistic expressions. Indeed, the claim that ostensive definition belongs to grammar is itself a statement about the *grammatical form* of the expression "ostensive definition" and serves to dissolve illusions of sense deriving from its misinterpretation.

Similar considerations apply to the notion of logical syntax employed in the *Tractatus*. There is a question about whether the *Tractatus* is already committed to the view that content can only be fixed from within language, or whether it assumes the possibility of a sideways-on perspective on language and reality.[7] And there is a further question about whether the *Tractatus* employs the term "logical syntax" so that differences in mere content count as differences in logical syntax, or only differences in logicosyntactical form count as differences in logical syntax.[8] Yet regardless of how these questions are answered, it is clear that the *Tractatus* is interested in investigating the logicosyntactical *form* of linguistic expressions. This is confirmed by the fact that all the examples of the sort of equivocation that the *Tractatus* claims to be responsible for the problems of philosophy are *cross-categorical* and lead to a misunderstanding of the logicosyntactical *form* of the relevant expressions (TLP 3.323).

1.7 Locating the Following Discussion

The rest of this Element discusses two closely related issues: (a) how Wittgenstein characterizes a failure to make sense, and (b) how he thinks these failures can be overcome. The first question bears on Wittgenstein's conception of language; the second on his conception of philosophical critique. Two competing approaches will be discussed. Section 2 presents the view that unmasking illusions of sense requires a *theory of sense* laying out criteria of meaningfulness and presupposing a *factorizing conception of language*, according to which the overall capacity to make sense is composed of subcapacities that can be successfully exercised even if the whole capacity is not. Section 3 makes a case for taking Wittgenstein to reject such a conception of language and the correlative form of theory of sense. Section 4 shows how Wittgenstein's philosophical critique can coherently proceed without relying on any such theory. The discussion will focus mainly on the *Tractatus*, but it is meant to illustrate general points that apply also to the later work.

The approach recommended below incorporates some central tenets of commentators who describe themselves as "resolute readers" of Wittgenstein. Specifically, Section 3 attributes to the *Tractatus* a version of what such readers have dubbed the "austere conception of nonsense," and Section 4 draws on their

---

[7] For a relatively recent installment of the long-standing debate about this question, see Diamond (2006) and Hacker (2001) respectively.

[8] It is generally maintained that the latter is the case. See, for instance, Conant (2002, p. 405) and Schroeder (2017, p. 253).

accounts of Wittgenstein's conception of clarification. By contrast, the alternative approach presented in Section 2 can be plausibly ascribed to at least some of the commentators who present themselves as opponents of the resolute reading or are singled out as such by its advocates.

While the following discussion agrees with some distinctive claims advanced by resolute readers, it does not amount to a defense of such a reading. The expression "resolute reading," at least in its original connotation, refers to a program for reading the *Tractatus* that is based on a certain interpretation of its penultimate remark, where Wittgenstein says that the reader who understands him must eventually throw away the Tractarian ladder and recognize Wittgenstein's own propositions as nonsensical (TLP 6.54).[9] This injunction, the program maintains, must be understood "resolutely," without wavering about the fact that the propositions of the *Tractatus* are *really* meant to be recognized as nonsensical, and thus as saying nothing whatsoever. This is meant to rule out, most prominently, the "ineffabilist" interpretation of the *Tractatus*, which resolute readers take to be widespread in the secondary literature. According to the ineffabilist reading, the propositions of the *Tractatus* are meant to enable the reader to grasp a number of insights into the nature of language, thought, and reality that, given the theory of sense laid down in the book, cannot be meaningfully expressed, but that retain nonetheless a quasipropositional form – in the sense that they *would* be expressed by propositions if per impossible they could be expressed at all, and indeed would be expressed by the very propositions of the *Tractatus* if such propositions could count, by the very standards they lay down, as meaningful.

The resolute interpretation of Wittgenstein's conception of nonsense on the one hand, and the resolute interpretation of Wittgenstein's conception of clarification on the other, enter the economy of the resolute program in the following way: the former, as a way of specifying what Wittgenstein means, in TLP 6.54, when he says that his propositions must be recognized as nonsensical; and the latter, as an account of how Wittgenstein's philosophical critique can proceed in the absence of a theory of sense backing up its charges of nonsensicality, including the charges directed against his own propositions. The availability of this alternative sort of account of Wittgenstein's conception of philosophical critique is crucial for the resolute program, since part of what a resolute reading of TLP 6.54 is supposed to entail is that the propositions of the *Tractatus*, being nonsensical, neither express nor somehow manage to communicate any theory of sense.

---

[9] Arguably, the term "resolute reading" has undergone some shifts in meaning since its introduction; see Bronzo & Conant (2017).

While the exegetical proposals about nonsense and clarification advanced by resolute readers *can* be put in the service of the resolute program, they are not inseparable from it, because they do not entail that a resolute understanding of TLP 6.54 should be taken as a guide for reading the book. In Sections 3 and 4, I will draw on the proposals advanced by resolute readers about nonsense and clarification, but I will not commit myself to the feasibility of the resolute program.

In the rest of this Element, I will leave as open as possible how TLP 6.54 is to be dealt with. This does not mean that *any* reading of it is compatible with the claims I will make about the *Tractatus*. Specifically, an ineffabilist reading of TLP 6.54 – of the sort criticized by resolute readers – presupposes a conception of nonsense that is incompatible with the view I ascribe to the *Tractatus* in Section 3.

The claims I will make about the Tractarian conceptions of nonsense and clarification *may* be compatible with the resolute program, but only if they are supplemented with a plausible answer to a version of an objection commonly mounted against resolute readers. In order to support those exegetical claims, I will appeal to various passages of the *Tractatus*. On the face of it, those passages must mean something if they are to bear any evidential weight, but how can they do so, if they fall within the scope of TLP 6.54, and if their nonsensicality is construed resolutely, thereby excluding the idea that they can somehow be intelligible in spite of their official nonsensicality? If I endorsed the resolute program, I would need to answer this objection. One option would be to appeal to the distinction invoked by some resolute readers between the "frame" and the "body" of the work, according to which only the latter is supposed to be recognized as nonsensical. Thus, I could maintain that the passages I will rely on in my discussion of nonsense and clarification belong to the frame. However, the frame/body distinction has been widely criticized as unprincipled. Resolute readers have been accused of assigning to the frame all and only the passages that they take to support their own interpretation.[10] A different option, which would avoid this difficulty, would be to claim that the views about nonsense and clarification that I will ascribe to the *Tractatus* fall within the scope of TLP 6.54, but have only a *transitional* role – as themselves rungs of the Tractarian ladder to be ultimately thrown away. If I chose this second option, all I could claim about the exegetical merits of the views I will ascribe to the *Tractatus* about nonsense and clarification is that they occupy a comparatively high position in the Tractarian ladder.

---

[10] For an overview of the debate about the frame/body distinction, see Bronzo (2012). Significantly, one of the main proponents of the distinction has recently discarded it as "unhelpful" (Diamond 2019, p. 5).

My actual current position on TLP 6.54 does not require an answer to the aforementioned objection. In the past, I described myself as a resolute reader of the *Tractatus*, in a sense of the expression that entails taking TLP 6.54 as a guide for reading the book (Bronzo & Conant 2017, p. 192). However, I have since become increasingly skeptical about the resolute program, because I have come to doubt the possibility of *any* reading of TLP 6.54 which is both internally consistent and in tune with the rest of the book, especially in the sense of capturing (to use an admittedly vague expression) the *experience* of reading and working closely with the book. I am presently inclined to a critical stance toward TLP 6.54 along the following lines:

(a) the remark is right in raising an issue about the functioning of clarificatory language, namely language clarifying the functioning of language;

(b) part of what it excludes, and rightly so, is an ineffabilist construal of clarificatory language, for to take this use of language as conveying ineffable quasipropositional truths is precisely to misunderstand its logic by modelling it on the logic of empirical statements;

(c) but with regard to its *positive* contribution to the clarification of clarificatory language, to the effect that this is an essentially transitional use of language which must culminate in the recognition of its own nonsensicality, TLP 6.54 is simply a *bad remark*. A remark that does not succeed in its purpose, and that is better ignored than taken as a guide for reading the *Tractatus*.

Points (a) and (b) agree with the resolute program, while (c) disagrees with it. I will not further develop this proposal in this Element. I mentioned it only as an option left open by the following discussion.

This should suffice as an explanation of how the interpretation I will present in Sections 3 and 4 relates to the resolute reading. Another aspect of the following discussion which deserves comment is framing the topic in terms of "capacities." As stated in Section 1.1, this Element deals with Wittgenstein's conception of the contrast between sense and nonsense, construed as the successful and the failed exercises of the self-conscious capacity to say something that makes sense. In recent years, there have been several proposals, partly inspired by Kant, to give central significance to the notion of a capacity in dealing with traditional issues in epistemology, the philosophy of mind, and other areas of philosophy.[11] Yet, the (German equivalents of) the term "capacity" and its cognate expressions do not figure prominently in Wittgenstein's writings. There are three main reasons behind my choice to draw on that notion.

---

[11] See Rödl (2010), McDowell (2011), Kern (2017), Kimhi (2018), Conant (2020a).

First, capacities (of the sort discussed in this Element) are something that *we* have. Formulating the contrast between sense and nonsense in terms of capacities puts *us* – thinking and speaking subjects – at the center of the scene. Construed in this way, the contrast concerns a dimension of success and failure in human life. This way of presenting the issue will perhaps be uncontroversial in relation to the later Wittgenstein, since it is virtually uncontested that he takes the notions of *practice* and *use* – and thus, of the *subjects* who participate in practices and use linguistic expressions – to be crucial for understanding language, thought, and logic. Bringing in capacities in interpreting the early Wittgenstein may be more controversial. However, even though this is not always noticed or emphasized, the *Tractatus* too accords central importance to the language user in its treatment of sense, nonsense, and logic. When the *Tractatus* introduces the notion of "picture," it characterizes it as something that "we make to ourselves" (TLP 2.1). The notion of "use" or "application" plays a crucial role in the Tractarian conception of language (TLP 3.26–3.28, 3.5; see Section 3.5). And the whole point of philosophical clarification, for the *Tractatus*, is to overcome illusions of sense – that is, cases where we are not making sense, even if we *believe* we are (cf. TLP 5.4733) – which requires the presence of someone who is subject to those illusions.[12]

Secondly, construing the sense/nonsense distinction as one between the successful and the failed exercise of a capacity gives prominence to the restricted sense in which this Element discusses the notion of "nonsense": nonsense as a failure to make sense, rather than mere absence of sense. At the same time, the notion of a *self-conscious* capacity (as defined in Section 1.1) captures the idea that the failure in question takes the form of an illusion. Part of what it is to fail to make sense is to mistakenly take oneself to make sense.

Thirdly, the notion of a capacity provides theoretical resources for accounting for the unity of the successful and the unsuccessful case in a manner that

---

[12] The emphasis I place on these passages, in support of the legitimacy of framing the Tractarian discussion of sense and nonsense in terms of capacities, can raise the worry that my approach to the *Tractatus* is – by the *Tractatus'* own lights – psychologistic. "Psychologism" is a protean term of criticism. From the perspective of G. E. Moore, the early Russell, and a certain strand in Frege (namely, the strand that emerges most clearly in the essay "The Thought," where *Gedanken* are characterized as mind-independent entities), any conception of content and logic that ascribes an essential role to the mind is guilty of psychologism (see Hylton 1990, Part II). I assume here that the *Tractatus* breaks with this tradition. (For some arguments, see Bronzo 2019). An appeal to capacities would indeed be psychologistic, for both early and later Wittgenstein, if it tried to derive the distinction between sense and nonsense from empirical generalizations about what people *take* to make sense. However, this is completely alien to the present approach. The notion of "capacity to make sense" that I employ in this Element comes together with the contrast between its successful and failed exercise. This is not derivable from what people *take* to make sense, since as explained in Section 1.1, when we fail to make sense, we nonetheless take ourselves to make sense.

incorporates a disjunctivist claim I will ascribe to Wittgenstein (Section 3.5). However, the bare notion of a capacity does not *entail* that particular account of the unity between the successful and the unsuccessful case, and remains therefore suitable for presenting without prejudice the rival position.

2 Appealing to a Theory of Sense

2.1 Theories of Sense and the Factorizing Conception of Language

It is natural to think that if a person (say, a philosopher) takes a certain sentence to make sense, and another person (say, Wittgenstein) claims that it makes no sense, then the second person has to offer reasons in support of their claim. A "theory of sense" – as the expression will be used henceforth – embodies a particular conception of what giving reasons in support of a nonsensicality charge can amount to.[13]

The goal of such a theory is to provide a *nonsensicality test*: we feed in some input, apply the test, and reach a verdict. The input consists of linguistic constructions that include, or are exhausted by, apparently meaningful sentences.[14] The test consists of conditions that the input must satisfy in order to be a meaningful sentence. Some theories of sense purport to specify necessary and sufficient conditions for being a meaningful sentence, while others purport to specify only necessary conditions. In the former case, what passes the test is a meaningful sentence; in the latter, it may or may not be. In either case, what fails the test is not a meaningful sentence. Thus, theories of sense that specify only necessary conditions can still have critical bite by excluding some apparently meaningful sentence as nonsensical.

It is essential to the present notion of a theory of sense that the input to be tested be specifiable *in neutral terms*, independently of the verdict. Otherwise, the whole procedure would be pointless, since the formulation of the question ("Does this sentence make sense or not?") would already contain the answer. The point is perhaps clearer if expressed in set-theoretic terms. A theory of sense is meant to carry out a partition of the set of all its possible inputs into a subset whose elements satisfy the conditions it specifies and a subset whose elements do not satisfy those conditions. However, the conditions for belonging

---

[13] The following characterization of a "theory of sense" should be taken as stipulative. I believe it fits some common uses of the expression or its analogues – such as "theory of meaning" or "theory of meaningfulness" – but this is inessential to our purposes.

[14] Depending on the theory, the input may also include linguistic constructions that do not appear in any way to be meaningful sentences, such as word salads. In such cases, the theory plays no role as a device for unmasking illusions of sense, since there is no illusion of sense to unmask to begin with.

to the set of possible inputs must be independent of the extra conditions that decide whether something belongs to one subset or the other.

At the level of the capacities of the language user, theories of sense are committed to the view that the capacity to use language to make sense must be factorizable into at least one subcapacity whose successful exercise does not involve the simultaneous successful exercise of the more encompassing capacity. The successful exercise of the subcapacity is what produces the input to which the test is applied. On pain of hindering the point of the testing procedure, it must be indifferent, for any successful exercise of the subcapacity, whether it *also* amounts to the successful exercise of the capacity to make sense. Whether the whole capacity to use language to make sense is successfully exercised depends on the satisfaction of extra conditions that leave untouched the identity of the particular exercises of the subcapacity. Thus, successful exercises of the subcapacity are identifiable across successful and failed exercises of the capacity to make sense, without any reference to whether they amount to the one or the other. In this sense, they constitute a *common factor* between making sense and failing to do so. In order to refer to this feature of theories of sense, I shall say that they presuppose a *factorizing conception of language*.[15]

The term "theory" is normally associated to the idea of systematicity, but this is not a crucial feature of theories of sense as presently defined. To take an extreme case, a view that specified the set of sentences that pass the nonsensicality test *by mere enumeration* would still count as a theory of sense in the present connotation, as long as the input of the test is specified independently of its outcome. Thus, the nonsystematicity or antisystematicity that is often ascribed to later Wittgenstein does not entail that he was not committed to a theory of sense.

Similarly, in both his early and later writings, Wittgenstein maintained that philosophy is not a "theory" (Section 1.4), but this does not entail that he was not committed to a theory of sense. One can ascribe to Wittgenstein a theory of sense and yet argue that it does not count as a "theory" in the sense that Wittgenstein finds problematic – for instance, because it is by its own lights ineffable, or because it consists of rules rather than statements, or because it consists of "reminders" conveying no new information. The choice of the label "theory of sense" is here meant to leave open the tenability of such readings. As I shall argue below, there are indeed reasons to maintain that Wittgenstein

---

[15] These characterizations of "common factor" and "factorizing conception of language" should be taken as stipulative. The terminology is derived from John McDowell, who employs it in other philosophical contexts (see, for example, McDowell 1998). I believe that the characterizations just given are faithful to McDowell's own understanding of the terminology, but this is inessential to the present discussion.

rejected theories of sense, but this is not a conclusion that can be swiftly reached by arguing along the following lines: a) Wittgenstein opposed philosophical theories; b) A theory of sense is a theory; c) Hence, Wittgenstein opposed theories of sense.

2.2 Theories of Sense and Wittgenstein Scholarship

It has often been assumed that Wittgenstein based his claims about the nonsensicality of apparently meaningful sentences on some theory of sense. Much of the disagreement among interpreters has hinged on which particular theory of sense should be attributed to Wittgenstein at which particular stage of his career.[16] The next three sections discuss three theories of sense that have been ascribed to the *Tractatus*. These three theories, taken together, illustrate a general framework for understanding most theories of sense that have been attributed to Wittgenstein, both early and late. They exemplify the three main options for construing the neutrally specifiable common factor between meaningful and nonsensical sentences to be tested for nonsensicality. The test can be taken to apply to:

a) *Contentful sentences*, some of which count as nonsensical in virtue of features of their content.
b) *Combinations of meaningful words*, some of which count as nonsensical in virtue of the meanings of the words and the way they are combined.
c) *Combinations of mere linguistic signs*, some of which count as nonsensical in virtue of the rules governing their employment.

These three options will be related, respectively, to the reading of "bipolarity" advanced by Elizabeth Anscombe (Section 2.3); to the readings of logical syntax proposed independently by David Pears and Hans-Johann Glock (Section 2.4); and to the reading of logical syntax presented by Peter Hacker (Section 2.5). Prioritizing accuracy over simplicity, I will also show that the readings of some of these commentors present strands pulling in other directions.

In order to see the generality of the three options just mentioned, one must bear in mind that there is ample room for variation with regard to the specification of the nonsensicality test (which may invoke, say, verifiability or pragmatic aptness instead of bipolarity or syntactical well-formedness), and with regard to additional characterizations of the neutral input to which the test is meant to be applied (which may include, say, also features of the context of utterance).

---

[16] These claims about Wittgenstein's scholarship can be challenged (see note 70). The following sections make a case for their plausibility.

Section 2.6 discusses the extent to which the same framework fits Peter Hacker's interpretation of grammar in the later Wittgenstein.

2.3 Bipolarity

For the *Tractatus*, a senseful proposition (*sinnvoller Satz*) is a sentence that is true in some circumstances and false in other equally possible circumstances. In the terminology of pre-Tractarian writings, senseful propositions are "bipolar": they have a true and a false pole (NL 288, NB 123). Bipolarity has often been taken to be part of a criterion of meaningfulness that is used by the *Tractatus* for excluding apparently meaningful sentences as nonsensical. On the most natural way of construing the bipolarity test, it applies to *contentful sentences*. Sentences that fail the test do not count as saying anything according to the technical notion of "saying" allegedly defined by the Tractarian theory. Yet they still say something according to a nontechnical notion of saying, because it is precisely in virtue of their content that they fail the test. They fail the test because *what they say* (in a nontechnical sense of the term) cannot be true as well as false.

Elizabeth Anscombe, in her classic study (1963), proposed a reading of this sort. According to Anscombe, the *Tractatus* holds that an apparently meaningful sentence is nonsensical if it is not (1) a bipolar proposition, or (2) a tautology or contradiction, or (3) a mathematical equation (p. 78). On Anscombe's reading, tautologies/contradictions and equations are neither bipolar senseful propositions nor nonsensical pseudopropositions. The bipolarity test is therefore qualified, but apart from those two exceptions, any nonbipolar sentence is nonsensical.[17]

According to Anscombe, sentences that fail the qualified bipolarity test include two remarkably different groups. The first group consists of sentences that express *insights*, but do not admit of intelligible negations, since the attempt to negate them results in mere confusion. The sentences in question are attempts to say what for the *Tractatus* is "shown" by senseful propositions and their limiting cases, that is, tautologies and contradictions. In order to characterize their status, Anscombe introduces a distinction (not explicitly present in the *Tractatus*) between two forms of saying: saying "informatively" and saying "illuminatingly" (1963, pp. 84–85). Even though the sentences under discussion cannot "informatively say" what is shown by senseful sentences and their limiting cases, they can "illuminatingly say" it. By pretheoretical criteria, they are perfectly intelligible and indeed true sentences. However, according to the

---

[17] For a detailed discussion of Anscombe's qualifications of the bipolarity test, and of the tensions they create in her reading of the *Tractatus*, see Diamond (2019).

theory of sense propounded by the *Tractatus*, which Anscombe considers to be unreasonably restrictive, they must be classified as nonsensical, since they are neither bipolar senseful propositions (which say informatively how things stand), nor tautologies/contradictions, nor mathematical equations. In addition to this first group of sentences failing the qualified bipolarity test, there are sentences that, when thought through, dissolve into incoherence. These are not illuminatingly nonsensical. They do not say – either informatively or illuminatingly – or show anything (Anscombe 1963, pp. 78–79, 85, 162–165).

Anscombe illustrates the distinction with the example, "'Someone' is not the name of someone." The sentence is meant to draw attention to the difference between the logical behavior of the word "someone" (in the common use that would be expressed in modern logical notation by means of variable and quantifier) and that of a proper name. The difference becomes evident when we reflect, for instance, on the fact that while "everybody loves *Mary*" entails that there is a universally loved person, "everyone loves *someone*" does not carry that implication. According to Anscombe, the sentence at issue is "obviously true" and "appears quite correct," but is not bipolar, since "its contradictory, when examined, peters out into nothingness." At the same time, it is neither a tautology nor an equation. Thus, Anscombe concludes, it is nonsensical by Tractarian standards. Both the sentence and its attempted negation count for the *Tractatus* as nonsensical, but while the latter is "only confusion and muddle," the former is "an insight" (pp. 84–85). The *Tractatus* cannot take the sentence to be true, since it classifies it as nonsensical. But on Anscombe's reading, it takes it to direct our attention to one of "the things which, though they cannot be 'said,' are yet 'shewn' or 'displayed'" by senseful propositions and their limiting cases – things that "it would be right to call ... 'true' if, *per impossibile*, they could be said" (p. 162).

Even though there are two kinds of sentences failing the qualified bipolarity test – those illuminatingly nonsensical and those dissolving into mere confusion – the test is powerless with sentence of the second kind. It cannot show that, when thought through, they peter out into nothingness. It cannot show, for example, that "'Someone' *is* the name of someone" expresses a mere confusion and that this is the reason why it is nonsensical. Conversely, once a sentence is shown to express only confusion, the test is superfluous: no theory of sense is required to conclude that it is nonsensical. Thus, the test can fulfil its function only when applied to sentences that do express, by pretheoretical standards, some sort of sense. This is the common factor between sense and nonsense to which the test can be applied and yield a result.[18]

---

[18] Verificationist readings of the *Tractatus* are structurally analogous to Anscombe's, in so far as they take the *Tractatus* to exclude some sentences as nonsensical because *what they (pretheoretically) say* is not verifiable.

2.4 Logical Syntax, As Applied to Meaningful Signs

One may attribute to the *Tractatus* a theory of sense based on rules of logical syntax, construed as rules for the combination of meaningful words. On such a theory, some apparently meaningful sentences are actually nonsensical because they consist of meaningful expressions combined in a manner that violates the rules of logical syntax, even though they comply with the surface-syntactical rules of ordinary grammar. Such sentences are nonsensical *in virtue of* the meanings of their parts and their mode of combination. The common factor between meaningful and nonsensical sentences to which the logicosyn-tactical test is applied is a combination of meaningful expressions. Logical syntax spells out the conditions that this common factor must satisfy in order to count as a meaningful sentence.

There are interpretations that come close to ascribing to the *Tractatus* a theory of sense of this sort, even though they are often committed to additional exegetical claims that pull in other directions. Two apposite examples are the readings advanced by David Pears and Hans-Johann Glock.

According to Pears, the basic constituents of sentences (Tractarian "names") get attached to the basic constituents of reality (Tractarian "objects" or "things"). Some combinations of objects are possible and other impossible. The objects determine whether the corresponding combinations of names are meaningful or nonsensical. Impossible combinations of objects correspond to nonsensical combinations of names. As Pears puts it: "Once a name has been attached to an object the nature of the object takes over and controls the logical behavior of the name, causing it to make sense in some sentential contexts but not in others" (Pears 1987, p. 88; see also Pears 2007, chap. 1). This passage implies that some combinations of names are nonsensical *because* of their meanings and mode of combination. So far, Pears' interpretation is a faithful illustration of the reading outlined above.

However, in an attempt to accommodate the Tractarian version of the Context Principle ("[O]nly in the context of a proposition has a name meaning," TLP 3.3), Pears introduces an important qualification. Names are supposed to retain their meanings only as long as they are combined in a manner that complies with the combinatorial possibilities of the things they stand for: "If this condition is not met, contact is broken and the name no longer represents the thing" (Pears 1987, p. 75). This implies that the names composing a nonsensical sentence are meaningless. Consequently, the common factor between a meaningful and a nonsensical sentence cannot be a combination of meaningful expressions. The qualification, therefore, distances Pears' interpretation from the aforemen-tioned sort of reading, but it is doubtful that the qualification and the claim it is supposed to qualify are mutually consistent. How can the nonsensicality of a combination of names be "caused" (as Pears puts it) by the things they name, if they do not indeed name those things? Pears speaks of the name-thing correlation as being "broken" or "annulled" in nonsensical contexts (p. 87). This suggests that some substitute of the correlation – something like its memory or shadow – is operative in nonsensical contexts: a substitute that does the job of the original (namely, determining the nonsensicality of the combination), without actually being the original. Yet it is hard to see what substance can lie behind this way of speaking.

Glock's reading is very clear about the fact that meaningful and nonsensical sentences can share combinations of meaningful expressions. According to Glock, "both early and late, [Wittgenstein] allowed that nonsense can result ... from combining meaningful expressions in a way that is prohibited by the rules for the use of these expressions" (Glock 2004, p. 222). Glock's name for this alleged sort of nonsense is "combinatorial nonsense" (2004, p. 235; 2015, p. 111). An example he offers is the sentence "Point x, y is C-flat." The *Tractatus*, he maintains, would regard it as nonsensical because its constituents have "incompatible meanings": being C-flat is not something that can be meaningfully predicated of a geometrical point (Glock 1996, p. 260). Glock also holds that the rules of logical syntax, for the *Tractatus*, "determine whether a combination of signs is meaningful" (1996, p. 76; see also p. 259) and identifies the "logical-syntactical category" of a Tractarian name with its "combinatorial possibilities" (p. 214). Thus, it seems clear that on Glock's reading of the *Tractatus*, combinatorial nonsense arises when expressions are combined in ways that violate the rules of logical syntax. Glock acknowledges that some aspects of the *Tractatus* appear to undermine the possibility of combinatorial nonsense (most prominently, its version of the Context Principle), but maintains that this is at most the sign of a tension in the *Tractatus* (1996, pp. 259–260; 2004, p. 228).

Glock emphasizes that the idea of combinatorial nonsense does not imply that some sentences are nonsensical because they express the wrong sort of sentential content – an "illogical thought," or an "impossible possibility," or a "senseless sense." In so far as some passages in Wittgenstein's corpus suggest that he thought otherwise, this was for Glock a false step (2004, pp. 237–238). This marks an important difference between Glock's reading and Anscombe's, which is indeed committed, as argued above, to the idea of sentences that are nonsensical in virtue of their content.

The claim that a sentence can be nonsensical because its parts have "incompatible meanings," combined with the assertion that logical syntax "determine whether a combination of signs is meaningful," constitute strong evidence that

Glock proposes a version of the reading outlined at the beginning of this section: the rules of logical syntax articulate a theory of sense that classifies some sentences as nonsensical on the basis of the meanings of their parts and their manner of combination. The evidence is strengthened by an apparent point of agreement with Pears. Like Pears, Glock maintains that for the *Tractatus* "correlating a name with an object determines the former's combinatorial possibilities" (1996, p. 301; see also p. 347). However, at some points Glock appears to take a different route. He holds that for the *Tractatus* the rules of logical syntax "are exclusively concerned with the combination of signs and make no reference to meaning, that is, semantics" (1996, p. 225), and that "we cannot derive the rules governing the use of a sign from its meaning, since the sign does not have a meaning in advance of these rules" (p. 239; see also p. 333). This suggests the following rather different picture: the rules of logical syntax govern the combination of *mere signs* and render them capable of being correlated with objects, and thus capable of acquiring a meaning, because they mirror their combinatorial possibilities. If this is Glock's well-considered view, the semantic common factor he posits between meaningful sentences and combinatorial nonsense plays no role in the nonsensicality test and the theory of sense he ascribes to the *Tractatus* falls under the heading of the next section.

2.5 Logical Syntax, As Applied to Mere Signs

A different way of understanding Tractarian logical syntax as a theory of sense is to take its rules to apply to mere signs instead of meaningful signs. These rules determine which combinations of linguistic signs are well-formed. If a given combination is a well-formed sentence, *and* all its components have been assigned a meaning, the sentence is meaningful. The theory provides only a necessary condition for making sense, but a sufficient condition for failing to do so: any apparently meaningful sentence that fails the test can be classified as nonsensical.

Arguably, the reading of Tractarian logical syntax proposed by Peter Hacker is a version of this interpretation. According to Hacker, "Wittgenstein thought that logical syntax as conceived in the *Tractatus* ... consist[s] of general rules that lay down which combinations of words are licensed and which excluded. In so doing they determine the bounds of sense, fixing what makes sense and what is nonsense" (Hacker 2003, p. 13). Hacker emphasizes, like Glock, that on his reading Wittgenstein never maintained that a nonsensical sentence expresses a wrong sort of sense (p. 9). Thus, logical syntax does not supply a test for determining whether a sentence, in virtue of the *content* it expresses, counts as meaningful or nonsensical. However, unlike Glock, Hacker maintains that the

Tractatus rejects combinatorial nonsense: sentential parts cannot have a meaning if they are put together in an illegitimate way. For Hacker, this is an unfortunate consequence of the peculiarities of the Tractarian conception of meaning, and especially of its adherence to an untenably strict version of the Context Principle (p. 17). Like Glock, Hacker maintains that one *should* admit combinatorial nonsense: their disagreement concerns only where the *Tractatus* stands on this issue. Thus, on Hacker's reading, the common factor between a meaningful and a nonsensical sentence to which the logicosyntactical test is applied is not a combination of meaningful words, but a combination of mere linguistic signs.

It is instructive to consider an example. For Hacker, the *Tractatus* holds that the sentence "red is a color" is nonsensical because "ill formed," and ill formed because it "contain[s] a formal concept, i.e. an unbound variable, in the role of a material one" (Hacker 2017, p. 216). The "unbound variable" at issue is the word "color" (p. 213). The idea is that there are rules governing the word "color" and rules governing the other parts of the sentence which forbid their combination. The rules would allow combinations in which the variable-word "color" is bounded, such as "There are two colors on the screen," and combinations of "red is" with material concept-words, such as "red is beautiful." Now, "unbound variable" and "word for a material concept" are names of categories of expressions, membership in which is determined by legitimate intersubstitutability. For Hacker, these are indeed *logicosyntactical* categories, but a logicosyntactical category, as I understand his reading, has no intrinsic connection with meaning.[19] It is simply a class of signs (whose identity in no way depends on their having a meaning) that (a) are intersubstitutable according to the combinatorial rules to which they are subject, and (b) belong to a system that happens to share the combinatorial possibilities of the elements of reality and is thereby fit to represent it.[20] If one formulated rules for the combination of basic decorative patterns for the purpose of wallpaper design, and such rules happened to mirror the combinatorial possibilities of the elements of reality, the decorative patterns would belong to "logicosyntactical categories" in Hacker's sense. The rules of logical syntax provide a test for determining whether

---

[19] Hacker writes about Tractarian names: "Names belonging to the same category have the same logical form, are governed by the same rules of logical syntax stipulating their combinatorial possibilities" (Hacker 1986, p. 33).

[20] For Hacker's account of the Tractarian doctrine of the isomorphism between language and reality, see Baker & Hacker (2005, p. 27) and Baker & Hacker (2009, p. 85). Crucially, the isomorphism is supposed to obtain between systems (language and reality) that are fully specifiable independently of each other. For a clear formulation of the reading of logical syntax that I am here ascribing to Hacker, see Johnston (2007, p. 388–389).

a combination of empty signs is potentially meaningful or irredeemably non-sensical, relative to those rules.[21]

2.6 Grammatical Rules

Like early Wittgenstein's logical syntax, later Wittgenstein's grammar has often been taken to articulate a theory of sense. Peter Hacker has defended this interpretation in many influential works, some of which he coauthored with Gordon Baker. As they put it in a characteristic passage:

> Grammar, as Wittgenstein understood the term, is the account book of language ... Its rules determine the limits of sense. By carefully scrutinizing usage from case to case, the philosopher may determine at what point he has drawn an overdraft on Reason, failed to conform with rules for the use of an expression, and so, in subtle and not readily identifiable ways, transgressed the bounds of sense. (Baker & Hacker 2009, p. 59)[22]

The fact that they ascribe to Wittgenstein a theory of sense (as defined in Section 2.1) becomes particularly clear when they claim that he countenanced "deductively valid arguments ... the premises of which spell out conditions of sense and the conclusion of which is that a given form of words lacks sense (since it fails to accord with the conditions of sense)" (Baker & Hacker 2005, p. 294). Here they ascribe to Wittgenstein a nonsensicality test. One feeds in a certain form of words, applies the test, and reaches a deductively valid verdict. The conditions of sense are specified by grammatical rules for the use of linguistic expressions, and the material to be tested consists of combinations of linguistic expressions.

It is clear that the grammatical test, for Hacker, does not apply to contentful sentences, since he emphasizes that Wittgenstein continued to reject the idea that sentences can be nonsensical because they express an impossible or illegitimate sentential content (Hacker 2000a, p. 90), but does the test apply to combinations of *meaningful* expressions, or to combinations of *mere* expressions? We saw that, according to Hacker, the Tractarian exclusion of combinatorial nonsense is due to unwarranted assumptions (Section 2.5). Such assumptions, on his reading, were rejected by later Wittgenstein. For later Wittgenstein, nonsensical forms of words can be "composed of significant expressions" (p. 98). But a meaningful word, on Hacker's reading, is simply a word that is governed by grammatical rules for its use. The grammatical rules for the use of a word "constitute its meaning" (p. 84). Thus, the nonsensicality of a sentence is supposed to be established exclusively on the basis of the words

---

[21] For an instructive discussion of Hacker's interpretation, see Vanrie (2017, chap. 1).

[22] See also Hacker (2003, p. 13) and Baker & Hacker (2005, p. 145–146). The image of grammar as the account book of language is Wittgenstein's (BT 58/48).

involved and the relevant grammatical rules: the meanings of the words, being constituted by the grammatical rules, play no additional role. The "forms of words" to be tested should therefore be understood as combinations of mere linguistics signs. In this respect, the grammatical theory of sense that Hacker ascribes to the later Wittgenstein preserves the structure of the logicosyntactical theory of sense that he ascribes to the *Tractatus*.[23]

Arguably, Hacker's interpretation of Wittgenstein's conception of grammar pulls sometimes in other directions. At some points, he maintains that the demonstration of the nonsensicality of a sentence is essentially a dialogical matter, for one must determine how the utterer of the sentence is using his words: "One must get his assent that *this* is the way he is using such-and-such an expression" (Hacker 2000a, p. 99). On this basis, Hacker asserts that "if philosophy is to be the guardian of the bounds of sense, it is a referee who can adjudicate only with the consent of the players, who acknowledge the particular rules according to which they use words" (p. 96). This changes considerably the focus of a demonstration of nonsensicality. Most of the action will happen at the very beginning, when one seeks to establish the premises of the deductive argument issuing in a verdict of nonsensicality. Taking for granted that one can neutrally identify the mere "form of words" that someone has uttered (a step that, as we shall see in the next section, is already controversial), one needs to establish by which grammatical rules they are meant to be governed. Only at that point will one be in a position to determine whether they accord with those rules, but once the allegedly preliminary steps have been taken, it is questionable that there is any substantive work to be done. To agree that we are using words according to certain rules is the same as agreeing that we are using the words correctly in some circumstances and incorrectly in some other circumstances. Thus, if we are in fact using the words incorrectly, our failure to realize it can only be a matter of distraction or some other readily identifiable mistake. The real locus of the controversy between the "guardian of the bounds of sense" and the alleged transgressor will therefore happen *before* the former has a chance to draw their nonsensicality inferences, when the two are still debating about how the alleged transgressor intends to use their words. If this is correct, the moments in Hacker's corpus to which I have just drawn attention lean toward the alternative exegetical approach to be discussed in Section 4, according to which philosophical clarification, as Wittgenstein conceived it, does not rely on any theory of sense.

---

[23] For Hacker's account of the differences between logical syntax and grammar, see the exchange between Dobler (2013) and Hacker (2013).

3 Undermining Theories of Sense

3.1 Theories of Sense and the Tractarian Conception of Language

We saw that theories of sense presuppose a factorizing conception of language (Section 2.1). For such theories to be viable, it must be possible to divide the overall capacity to use language to make sense into a number of subcapacities that may be successfully exercised independently of the successful exercise of the more encompassing capacity. These subcapacities must be posited in order to have a neutrally specifiable input to which the nonsensicality test can be applied.

On a *nonfactorizing* conception of language, while it is possible to discern various aspects in the exercise of the capacity to use language to make sense, none of these aspects is extractable from the phenomenon they characterize. When one fails to make sense, the failure affects all the dimensions of the linguistic performance. There is no way of identifying an aspect of one's linguistic performance while bracketing the question of whether it amounts to a case of making sense or rather to a case of failing to do so. Thus theories of sense, in so far as they are meant to apply to performances belonging to the order of language, will be superfluous. They are bound to enter the scene too late, when the question they aim to answer has already been settled.

A significant portion of Wittgenstein scholarship has challenged the idea that he subscribed to a factorizing conception of language, even though the challenge has often concerned particular instances of such a conception, rather than the conception in its full generality. This section outlines a nonfactorizing interpretation of the Tractarian conception of language, combining and elaborating contentions characteristically advanced by commentators associated to the resolute reading of the book. It examines the relation between sentential and subsentential meaning (Sections 3.2–3.3), between semantic content and logicosyntactical categories (Section 3.4), and between meaningful signs and mere signs (Section 3.5). At each step of this progression, it will be shown that the nonfactorizing reading undermines the ascription to the book of a whole set of theories of sense. The conclusion will be that, for such theories to have a foothold, they must construe the material to be tested as something lying outside the linguistic order altogether – say, as a merely acoustic or geometrical phenomenon. Yet this is not what theories of sense normally do, and for good reasons, because the prospects for theories of sense of this sort are highly doubtful (Section 3.6). The section will end by connecting this interpretation to the conception of nonsense ascribed to the *Tractatus* by resolute readers (Sections 3.7 and 3.8). I believe it can be shown that Wittgenstein continued to reject the factorizing conception of language in his later works, but this is not something I can argue for in this Element.[24]

It should be emphasized that the interpretation of the Tractarian conception of language presented below is controversial, both exegetically and philosophic- ally. Virtually any passage that will be adduced in its support is liable to a variety of other interpretations. The aim here is not to resolve the relevant controverses, but only to present an exegetical option, support it with some plausible textual evidence, and spell out its implications for the possibility of theories of sense. The main text that we shall consider is the "chapter" of the *Tractatus* consisting of TLP 3.3 and its subordinate propositions.

3.2 The Context Principle and Subsentential Meaning

TLP 3.3 contains a version of the Context Principle, which concerns the relationship between sentential and subsentential meaning. Its standard formu- lation is normally ascribed to Gottlob Frege: "It is only in the context of a proposition that words really have any meaning" (Frege 1980, §62). With evident reference to Frege, the *Tractatus* says: "only in the context of a proposition has a name meaning" (TLP 3.3). Names for the *Tractatus* are the constituents of elementary propositions, out of which all other propositions are constructed. Thus, we are told that a name has meaning – which for *Tractatus* is the same as standing for an object, also called its "meaning" (TLP 3.203) – only in the context of a proposition or sentence (*Satz*).[25]

This is enough to rule out the idea that names may have a meaning in isolation. The dictum opposes therefore a familiar sort of semantic atomism according to which meaningful sentential components enter the propositional nexus only incidentally. What the dictum amounts to, however, depends cru- cially on what the *Tractatus* means in this context by "proposition" (*Satz*). The book uses the term in various ways. Sometimes it is clearly restricted to "*senseful* propositions" (*Sinnvolle Sätze*), picturing contingent situations (e.g., TLP 4.021–4.024).[26] Other times it covers also "pseudo-propositions" such as tautologies and mathematical equations, which misleadingly appear to picture contingent situations, but fulfil instead other functions (e.g., TLP 6.1, 6.2). And yet other times it is used to include also "nonsensical pseudopropositions" (TLP 4.1272), involving a failure to picture contingent situations (TLP 6.54). In the context of TLP 3.3, it is reasonable to assume that the term refers to senseful

---

[24] For some arguments about later Wittgenstein, see Bronzo (2017) and Conant (2020b).

[25] This version of the Context Principle can also be found, arguably, in TLP 2.0122, 2.13–2.131, 3.22, and 3.314.

[26] A senseful proposition has the form: "Such and such is the case" (TLP 4.5). Of course, it can be negative. *What* it claims to be the case may be that things do *not* stand in a certain way.

propositions.[27] On this reading, the Tractarian version of the Context Principle says that names (i.e., propositional constituents) have meaning only in the context of senseful propositions, saying truly or falsely that something is the case. Since senseful propositions are essentially articulated into names (TLP 3.141), the view is that propositional and subpropositional meaning necessarily come together: saying something true or false requires referring to objects, and referring to objects is something that can be achieved only in the course of saying that something is the case. In contrast to atomistic, bottom-up accounts, the *Tractatus* champions a conception of the proposition as an organic unity whose parts make a distinctive contribution to the meaning of the whole in which they occur, and can occur in an indefinite number of other appropriate wholes, but cannot be separated from any such whole and subsist in isolation.

After stating its version of the Context Principle, the *Tractatus* goes on to clarify its content by introducing the notion of "symbol" (*Symbol*) or "expression" (*Ausdruck*), defined as "everything – essential for the sense of the proposition – that propositions can have in common with one another" (TLP 3.31). Symbols are also said to "characterize a form and a content" (TLP 3.31) and to be "the common characteristic mark[s] of a class of propositions" (TLP 3.311). Tractarian names, and more generally meaningful subsentential expressions (whether simple or complex), qualify as Tractarian symbols, along with complete senseful propositions, which are "limiting cases" of symbols (TLP 3.313). A subpropositional symbol is perspicuously presented by a "propositional variable," whole values are all the significant propositions whose senses depend on the meaning of the symbol in question (TLP 3.313). For example, assuming for the sake of illustration that the word "Socrates," taken to name a certain philosopher, counted as a Tractarian name, the proper way of displaying it would be a propositional variable such as " … Socrates …, " whose values are all the propositions in which the word is used to refer to that person.[28] The notation makes clear that subsentential semantic units are abstractable, but not extractable, from senseful propositions.[29]

Given what else happens in the *Tractatus*, one may ascribe to the book an implicit commitment to a less restrictive construal of the Context Principle. It is reasonably clear, for instance, that the names appearing in tautologies and contradictions are supposed to have a meaning, even though the wholes to which they

---

[27] For a different reading, taking the term to apply here also to *nonsensical* propositions, see Johnston (2007).

[28] The notation just employed does not appear in the *Tractatus*. It is taken from Morris (2008, p. 173).

[29] For a different interpretation of Tractarian symbols, which takes them to be individuated only by their logicosyntactical form and not also by their content, see Johnston (2007).

belong are not senseful. One can therefore generalize the notion of the sort of "whole" in which a name must occur in order to be meaningful so as to include the other complete meaningful uses of language envisioned by the *Tractatus* (see Section 1.3). In its generalized form, the principle would state that a name has meaning only in the context of a complete intelligible use of language. Arguably, there is no room in the *Tractatus* for the idea of a nonhierarchical plurality of complete uses of language: the picturing use remains the central one and all the others have a derivative status. But the *Tractatus* can insist on a fundamental distinction between (a) expressing a subsentential content, which is essentially *part* of doing something else, and (b) making a complete use of language, even though only the picturing use of language is not only complete, but also nonderivative.

The Context Principle – in both this generalized form and the more restricted version described in the 3.3s – rules out combinatorial nonsense, that is, the idea of a sentence that is nonsensical in virtue of the meanings of its parts and manner of composition (Section 2.4). By the same token, it opposes the factorization of our linguistic capacity into the capacity to make sense and an independent capacity to express subsentential meanings. A failure to make sense goes all the way down to subsentential meaning, involving *also* a failure to employ meaningful words. Thus, the principle undermines theories of sense purporting to specify conditions that a combination of meaningful expressions must satisfy in order to count as a meaningful sentence.

Just as the Tractarian versions of the Context Principle rule out combinatorial nonsense, they also rule out the idea of sentences that are nonsensical in virtue of the contents they express, and thus the possibility of theories of sense of the sort described in Section 2.3. For it is hard to see how a sentence composed of meaningless words could somehow manage to express any sort of sentential content, thought, or insight to which standards of sense could be applied.

3.3 The Context Principle, Compositionality, and Productivity

A standard objection to the dictum that words have meanings only in the context of meaningful sentences is that it seems incompatible with the compositionality and productivity of language. We are able to form and understand an indefinite number of sentences that we have never heard before (linguistic productivity). This obviously depends on the fact that the meanings of sentences are determined, at least partly, by the meanings of their parts and manner of composition (linguistic compositionality).[30] It would seem, therefore, that we understand

---

[30] I shall work here with this comparatively relaxed definition compositionality, which allows for a contribution of the context of utterance. But the conclusions I will reach apply also to a stricter definition of compositionality, according to which the meanings of sentences are determined *exclusively* by the meanings of their parts and manner of composition.

new sentences because we already know the meanings of their parts and the significance of their manner of combination (plus, perhaps, how the meanings of sentences depend on features of the context of utterance). However, doesn't this require that words have a meaning prior to and independently of the meanings of the sentences in which they occur? And isn't this precisely what is denied by the versions of the Context Principle ascribed above to the *Tractatus*?[31]

Three preliminary observations are in order. First, the Tractarian understanding of the Context Principle does not entail that words have no subsentential meanings of their own, or that words stand to sentences as letters stand to words. On the contrary, it rules out this absurd idea, since it lays out a condition *on the subsentential meaningfulness of words*. Secondly, the Tractarian understanding of the Context Principle is fully compatible with the claim that the meanings of sentences depend on, or are even fully determined by, the meanings of their parts. Hence, it is fully compatible with "linguistic compositionality," if this is all one means by the phrase.[32] Thirdly, the meaning of a subsentential expression, for the *Tractatus*, is not uniquely tied to any particular meaningful sentence in which it occurs. On the contrary, it is a unit that can *reoccur* unchanged in an indefinite number of *different* sentences. Meaningful subsentential expressions are working parts of meaningful sentences, and while they cannot subsist unless they are part of a meaningful sentence in which they fulfil their function, they can fulfil exactly the same function in an indefinite number of different sentences. This is part of what the *Tractatus* wants to bring out when it claims that a subsentential expression is properly presented by a "propositional variable" (Section 3.2).

These preliminary steps are insufficient to account for productivity, because they do not explain how the roles that words play in sentences already encountered bear on the roles they play in new sentences. One way to fill the lacuna without recanting the Tractarian commitment to the Context Principle is to introduce a distinction – not explicit in the *Tractatus* – between the *established* and the *actual* meaning of an expression. The established meaning of a word is a form of potentiality: it is the contribution that the word can make to the meanings of complete sentences, given the standing conventions of the language. The actual meaning of a word, by contrast, is the contribution that it

---

[31] The *Tractatus* emphasizes explicitly the productivity and compositionality of language (TLP 3.318. 4.24–4.03). Thus, the *Tractatus* faces not only the challenge of holding an untenable form of contextualism, but also of being internally inconsistency. I discuss this alleged inconsistency in Bronzo (2011).

[32] The Tractarian understanding of the Context Principle is incompatible with compositionality only if one builds into this notion the additional idea that the parts of a sentence have a meaning prior to and independently of the meaning of the whole.

makes (in actuality and not merely in potentiality) to the meaning of the complete sentence in which it occurs on a given occasion. In natural language, each word typically has various established meanings, even categorically different ones.[33]

Productivity can then be explained as follows. By default, words actualize on new occasions some of their established meanings – or ways of extending or modifying their established meanings that are themselves instantiations of established linguistic patterns. Arbitrary stipulations of new meanings for familiar words are parasitical phenomena. Thus, upon encountering what appears to be a sentence of a given language, one tries to make sense of the sentence in a way that accords with the range of established meanings of what appear to be its component words – or with the range of natural extensions or modifications of those meanings. The bite of the Context Principle, as the *Tractatus* understands it, is that none of those potentialities is actualized unless the whole sentence makes sense. Put otherwise: The hearer makes *hypotheses* about which established meanings are actualized by what they take to be occurrences of subsentential expressions of a particular language; but none of those hypotheses is confirmed unless they lead to a way of *making sense* of what the speaker is saying.[34]

On this elaboration of the Tractarian view, words carry their established meanings in both meaningful and nonsensical contexts. However, they can have actual meanings only in meaningful sentences. Given a nonsensical sentence, understood as the expression of an illusion of sense, one can identify the semantic functions that its parts *fail* to fulfil in that context, as well as the semantic functions that they *could* fulfil in other contexts in accordance with the standing conventions of the language. However, there is no semantic function that sentential parts *actually* fulfil in nonsensical contexts.[35]

The distinction between actual and established meaning can help to address another common objection to the Context Principle, to the effect that words have a meaning even when they occur "in isolation." One can compile a list of words of a given language and ask (say, during a language exam) what their meanings are. There are right and wrong answers, and doubts can be resolved by

---

[33] Here and below, I use the term "word" so that a word is not identified by its established or actual meaning. The same word may have, on any of its occurrences, many different established meanings; on different occurrences, different actual meanings; and on some of its occurrences, no actual meaning. A word, in this sense, is a special case of a Tractarian sign, as the notion is interpreted in Section 3.5.

[34] For a similar account of productivity, emphasizing the *conditional* nature of the assignment of subsentential meanings, see Diamond (1991, pp. 109–111).

[35] For a different way of mobilizing the actuality/potentiality distinction in connection with the interpretation of the Context Principle, leading to different conclusions about Wittgenstein's conception of nonsense, see Glock (2015).

consulting a dictionary. In order to accommodate this undeniable phenomenon without relinquishing the Tractarian understanding of the Context Principle, we can hold that the phenomenon concerns only the *established* meanings of words. It is possible to identify the established subsentential meanings of isolated words; but these potentialities are actualized only when the words make a contribution to the meanings of complete sentences.

On the present proposal, the Tractarian understanding of the Context Principle (in both of the versions described in the previous section) applies directly only to actual subsentential meaning. It does not apply in the same way to established subsentential meaning, since I have suggested that words can retain their established meanings when they occur in nonsensical contexts (where they *fail* to actualize specific established meanings), as well as when they occur in the sort of "isolation" illustrated by a list of words given during a language exam (where the words are not even *meant* to actualize any of their established meanings, because they are not meant to be used to make sense). However, the Tractarian understanding of the Context Principle applies in a different way to established subsentential meaning, because it contributes to defining *what it is*. Established subsentential meaning is a potentiality, and the Context Principle constrains what kind of potentiality it is. It is the potentiality to make a contribution to *making sense*.[36]

3.4 Logicosyntactical Categories

After the introduction of the notion of a "symbol" as something that character-izes *both the form and the content* of the significant propositions in which it occurs, the *Tractatus* goes on to point out that propositions may also share *purely formal* features. These, too, are perspicuously presented by propositional variables, whose values are all the propositions sharing the formal features:

> If we change a constituent part of a proposition into a variable, there is a class of propositions which are all the values of the resulting variable proposition. This class in general still depends on what, by arbitrary agreement, we mean by parts of that proposition. But if we change all those signs, whose meaning was arbitrarily determined, into variables, there always remains such a class. But this is now no longer dependent on any agreement; it depends only on the nature of the proposition. It corresponds to a logical form, to a logical prototype. (TLP 3.315)

The substitution of variables for constants corresponds to a process of abstraction (cf. RLF 162). Consider the senseful proposition "Socrates loves Plato." If

---

[36] There are common challenges to the Context Principle that I have not mentioned in this section and cannot address in this Element. For an overview, see Baker & Hacker (2005, p. 159).

we replace the last two expressions with variables, we obtain a propositional variable, say " $\Psi(\text{Socrates}, x)$," which displays a symbol characterizing the form and content of a class of propositions: "Socrates loves Plato," "Socrates hates Aristotle," etc. If we replace all the constant expressions in the original proposition with variables, we obtain a propositional variable, say " $\Psi(x, y)$," displaying a propositional form: the form shared by all the propositions stating that two objects stand in a certain dyadic relation. (For the sake of illustration, let's pretend here, and continue to pretend below, that "Socrates" and "Plato," as normally understood, could count as Tractarian names.) Thus, the logical form of a proposition is something that can only be found and seen *in* meaningful propositions. It can be singled out for special attention through a process of abstraction, but cannot be stripped out of meaningful propositions and subsist on its own.

The same holds for the logical form of subpropositional expressions. The variable " $\Psi(\text{Socrates}, x)$" does not present what is common to *all* the propositions in which the name "Socrates" stands for a certain person, since the name can also occur in propositions that do not state the obtaining of a dyadic relation. For instance, the name can occur in the proposition "Socrates is wise," whose form can be presented by means of the propositional variable " Φx." As mentioned in Section 3.2, the contentful subpropositional symbol "Socrates" is properly presented by a propositional variable such as "... Socrates ...," which abstracts not only from the other contentful features of the propositions whose sense it characterizes, but also from all the specificities of their form besides the fact that they are significant propositions containing that meaningful name. Now, if we take the variable "... Socrates ..." and replace *its* constant expression with another variable, we obtain a propositional variable, "... x ...," presenting the form of a name, in accordance with the Tractarian insistence that "[e]very variable can be conceived as a propositional variable ... [i]ncluding the variable name" (TLP 3.314). Thus, subpropositional logical form is only a feature of subpropositional contentful symbols, which are in turn only features of meaningful propositions.

The notion of logical form, as something that is singled out through abstraction from meaningful propositions, is intertwined with the idea of substitutability *salva significatione*. The fact that two symbols have the same logical form is expressed by the fact that they are values of the same propositional variable; and what all the values of a propositional variable have in common is that they can be substituted for one another in all propositional contexts without generating nonsense. But a logicosyntactical category, as construed by the *Tractatus*, is also defined by relations of substitutability *salva significatione* (Sections 1.5 and 1.6). On this basis, the notion of "logical form" described in the TLP 3.31s can be taken to coincide with the Tractarian notion of a logicosyntactical category.

This interpretation takes the *Tractatus* to oppose a factorization of our capacity to use language to make sense into a subcapacity to produce and combine logicosyntactical units. Logicosyntactical units cannot constitute a common factor between meaningful and nonsensical sentences, since an expression belongs to a logicosyntactical category only in so far as it also has a content and makes a contribution to the meaning of a complete sentence. Isolated subsentential expressions, or the parts of nonsensical sentences, can belong to logicosyntactical categories *in potentiality*, in accordance with the standing linguistic conventions; but such potentialities are *actualized* only when the expressions are working parts of meaningful sentences. Consequently, this interpretation undermines theories of sense purporting to sort out combinations of logicosyntactical units that can become meaningful sentences (if they are given a specific content in addition to a logicosyntactical form) from those that are doomed to nonsensicality.

This does not mean that the present interpretation of logicosyntactical categories suffices to refute the ascription to the *Tractatus* of the sort of theory of sense described in Section 2.5. In fact, the foregoing attacks such an ascription only with regard to its appropriation of the terminology of "logicosyntactical categories" and "rules of logical syntax." Yet even if one concedes that the *Tractatus* understands this terminology in the way explained in this section, one can still maintain that the *Tractatus* endorses a theory of sense of the following sort: There are rules for the combinations of linguistic signs that determine which combinations can become meaningful and which ones are irredeemably nonsensical – where the specification of linguistic signs, of their combinatorial categories, and of the relevant combinatorial rules can be achieved without any appeal to the notion of a meaningful sentence. In order to block this sort of reading, we need to question the conception of linguistic signs that it ascribes to the *Tractatus*.

3.5 Linguistic Signs

After introducing subsentential symbols and logical form as abstractions from meaningful sentences, the *Tractatus* goes on to define, in terms of symbols, the notion of *sign* (*Zeichen*): "The sign is what is sensibly perceptible in the symbol" (TLP 3.32).[37] A fundamental feature of the sign/symbol relation is that the same sign can be common to different symbols (TLP 3.321–3.323). For

---

[37] The same order of definition appears earlier in the book (TLP 3.1–3.11), where signs are first mentioned. For a discussion of these passages, see Bronzo (2017, p. 1343).

example, the sign "is" can be used to make different contributions to the sense of propositions, and belongs in each case to a different symbol – the copula, the sign of equality, and the expression of existence (TLP 3.323). A second feature of the sign/symbol relation is that it is mediated by the notion of *use*: "In order to recognize the symbol in the sign we must consider the significant use" (TLP 3.326). Which symbol a sign belongs to on any given occasion depends on how the sign is used on that occasion to say something that makes sense. Finally, a third feature of the sign/symbol relation is that a sign, on some of its occurrences, may not belong to any symbol, but amount to a *mere* sign. A nonsensical pseudoproposition is indeed composed of signs, but by signs that, in that linguistic context, *fail* to symbolize: they are apparently put to significant use, but are in fact devoid of both logical form and semantic content.[38]

Given these constraints about the sign/symbol relation, there are two fundamental exegetical options. One option – call it the *Additive Reading*[39] – holds that the *Tractatus* takes the notion of symbol to result from the combination of a prior and independent notion of sign and some extra ingredient. A symbol is a *sign plus use*, where neither the sign nor the relevant form of use presupposes what is supposed to result from their combination. On this reading, the conditions of identity of a Tractarian sign in no way depend on how the sign contributes to the expression of thoughts. A Tractarian sign is, accordingly, something like a repeatable geometrical shape or acoustic pattern. If one adopts this approach, there is still plenty of room to disagree about how to construe the sort of use that is supposed to turn a sign into a symbol. The long-standing debate between "mentalist" and "antimentalist" readings of the *Tractatus* takes place within the framework of this first exegetical option, in so far as it is understood as a debate about whether the sort of use that turns a sign into a symbol involves a mental act connecting the sign to an object or is instead only a matter of manipulating empty signs.[40]

The other option – call it the *Nonadditive Reading* – rejects the idea that a symbol is a prior and independent sign plus some extra ingredient. It is therefore characterized by a purely negative commitment. Of course, embracing this negative commitment does not yet amount to providing an account of the Tractarian conception of the sign/symbol relation. There is room for debate among advocates of the Nonadditive Reading about how to provide this positive

---

[38] For a different reading of nonsensical propositions, according to which they are composed of symbols rather than mere signs, see Johnston (2007).

[39] For a similar employment of this terminology, see Conant (2020b).

[40] This is how the debate is generally understood from the mentalist side. Arguably, some opponents of the mentalist approach criticize it *qua additive reading* and do not seek to replace it with another reading of that sort (see Bronzo 2017, pp. 1346–1347).

account. The task is far from trivial. Part of the difficulty is that a defensible proposal should explain not only (i) below, but also (ii) and (iii):

i) the same sign may belong to a symbol on some occasions and *fail* to belong to any symbol on other occasions;
ii) the same sign may belong to different symbols on different occasions;
iii) a sign that belongs to a symbol on some occasions may also occur in contexts where the speaker is *neither* using it to make sense, *nor* failing to use it to make sense.

Some cases discussed in the *Tractatus* that can appear to belong to (iii), such as displaying a word in order to explain what it means, can perhaps be dealt with by appealing to a broad notion of "making sense" that includes, along with the picturing use of language, also a host of derivative uses (Section 3.2). But there are cases that cannot be dealt with in this way. Consider, for example, copying down words in order to learn a new writing system, or composing words during a Scrabble game. To say that in such cases one is using language to "make sense" would be to stretch the notion of making sense beyond recognition; and it is equally clear that one is not *failing* to make sense in these cases, since one is not even trying to do so. While cases of this sort are not discussed in the *Tractatus*, a charitable reading of the book should not render them incompatible with its conception of linguistic signs.

Here I wish to recommend a version of the Nonadditive Reading, even though I am going to outline it only to the point of being able to account for the phenomenon that bears most directly on this Element – namely, the occurrence of signs that do not belong to any symbol because they occur in nonsensical pseudopropositions (i). The account will therefore be incomplete, and its exegetical viability will depend upon the possibility of extending it in a manner that can explain also (ii) and (iii).[41] It should also be emphasized that the account introduces a theoretical framework that is not explicitly present in the *Tractatus*. It is therefore a way of developing and systematizing Tractarian ideas in a manner that purports to remain consistent with the text, while going beyond the text as it stands.

---

[41] The notion of an "attenuated exercise" of a capacity, as developed in Conant (2020a), can prove useful for extending the account of Tractarian signs sketched below to (iii). Alternatively, one might explore the idea of successful exercises of derivative capacities. Conant's recent account of Tractarian signs (2020a, Section XIII) does not include a detailed explanation of how it can vindicate (ii) without relapsing into a version of the Additive Reading. Bronzo (2017) seeks to account for (ii) by construing the fact that different symbols can share the same sign in terms of the fact that different symbols can *misleadingly appear to be the same symbol*. Admittedly, the proposal does not shed sufficient light on the relevant notion of appearance.

The core of the proposal is that a sign is *either* the result of the successful exercise of our capacity to produce symbols, *or* the result of a failed exercise of that capacity. As the either-or formulation brings out, the account follows a *disjunctivist* schema.[42] This is arguably inevitable, for as soon as we construe a sign as an independently intelligible common factor between a symbol and a mere sign (where a "mere sign" is a sign that does not belong to any symbol), we are already operating within the framework of the Additive Reading. But the account is not based exclusively on a purely logical notion of disjunction, which as such can bring together completely unrelated items, as happens when we define, say, a "ftable" as what is either a table or a fable. On the present proposal, the unity of the two disjuncts is given by the notion of our fallible capacity to symbolize, which is successfully exercised in the case of the first disjunct, and unsuccessfully exercised in the case of the second disjunct.[43] The identity of the mere signs composing nonsensical pseudopropositions is given by the fact that they result from a *failure* to exercise our capacity to make sense in a linguistic, sensibly perceptible manner.

On this account, signs occur in both meaningful and nonsensical contexts, but there is no separate capacity to produce signs whose successful exercise results in a common factor between sense and nonsense. There is only the fallible capacity to produce symbols, whose successful exercises result in symbols, and whose unsuccessful exercises result in mere signs. Producing signs consists in exercising this fallible capacity, either successfully or unsuccessfully.

This proposal entails that the *Tractatus* rejects the possibility of the sort of theory of sense described in Section 2.5. That sort of theory presupposes that the occurrence of a linguistic sign can be identified in neutral terms, independently of whether it is successfully or unsuccessfully used to make sense. The theory is then supposed to formulate "rules of logical syntax" that specify necessary conditions for making sense, thereby excluding some arrangements of signs as irredeemably nonsensical, but on the version of the Nonadditive Reading just outlined, there is no room for such a neutral identification of linguistic signs. Whether something belongs to the disjunctively defined genus of a sign is determined by whether it belongs to one of the two disjuncts. We may *conjecture*, on the basis of context and sensible appearances, that we are witnessing the occurrence of a sign without yet taking a stance on whether it belongs to a case

---

[42] The background of the present discussion is especially the form of disjunctivist developed by John McDowell (1998, 2010, 2013).

[43] For the idea that disjunctivism, at least in the version developed by McDowell, is not based on the purely logical notion of disjunction, but relies crucially on the notion of capacity (to the point of making "disjunctivism" a misnomer), see Rödl (2010). The appeal to capacities has become more prominent in McDowell's recent discussions of disjunctivism (2010, 2013).

of making sense or failing to do so. But whether we are in fact witnessing the occurrence of a sign (rather than, say, a scratch or a decorative pattern), and which sign this is, is *settled* only by whether it is a certain symbol or instead the result of a failure to produce that symbol. On this view, therefore, conclusively identifying the occurrence of a sign already involves an answer to the question that the theory of sense described in Section 2.5 seeks to answer – namely, whether the sign belongs to a piece of nonsense or may instead belong to a meaningful sentence.

Admittedly, there is no unequivocal textual evidence in favor of the Nonadditive Reading, let alone for the specific version of the reading sketched above. It is clear that the author of the *Tractatus* had explicitly in mind the alternative between an atomistic and a nonatomistic conception of subsentential meaning and opted for the latter. It is also reasonably clear that he construed logical form (or at least *a* notion of logical form) as an abstraction from the meaningful employment of linguistic signs. But it is not equally clear that he had explicitly in mind the alternative between the additive and the nonadditive construal of linguistic signs and opted for the latter. The choice between the two exegetical approaches remains to a large extent a matter of interpretation, in the sense that it goes beyond what can be explicitly found in the text. Nevertheless, the Nonadditive Reading can be supported by the following considerations. 1) The *Tractatus* introduces the notion of sign *after* and *in terms of* the already introduced notion of symbol. This would be a rather idiosyncratic mode of presentation if Wittgenstein were endorsing an additive conception of linguistic signs. 2) The *Tractatus* never characterizes linguistic signs in a manner that conforms with the assumptions of the Additive Reading – for instance, as mere shapes or sounds.[44] 3) The *Tractatus* contains no clear account of what turns a sign into a symbol. Commentators have tried to fill out this alleged lacuna in various ways – normally by invoking mental acts, or ostensive definitions, or the manipulation of empty signs. Yet, the presence of such a lacuna remains surprising if the *Tractatus* is indeed endorsing an additive conception of the sign/symbol relation. This makes it reasonable to consider the possibility that there is in fact no such lacuna, because the *Tractatus* does not define a symbol in terms of a prior and independent notion of sign and some extra ingredient. 4) Finally, there are philosophical reasons to resist an additive conception of

---

[44] In a lecture delivered in 1930, according to the notes of his students John King and Desmond Lee, Wittgenstein presented the sign/symbol distinction and characterized a sign as "the written scratch or noise" (LWL 26). This can be adduced in support of the Additive Reading. However, that statement is absent from the notes from the same lecture taken by G. E. Moore. On Moore's account, Wittgenstein simply explained what he meant by "sign" with an example: "'Red' (the word) is a sign" (MWL 76). On the greater reliability of Moore's notes, see the editorial introduction to MWL.

linguistic signs. The standard definition of a phoneme in linguistics is not carried out in purely acoustic or articulatory terms, but makes essential reference to the meaningful use of language: a phoneme is generally understood as the minimal unit of language that makes a difference for the meanings of linguistic expressions.[45] However, there are reasons for being skeptical of the possibility of a reduction of phonology, construed as the study of phonemes, to phonetics, construed as the study of the sounds of language from a perspective and with a conceptual apparatus that eschews any essential reference to linguistic meaning. It is questionable, for instance, that we can in general specify what it is for the same phoneme to occur again in terms of purely acoustic or articulatory properties.[46] Similar observations apply to the written or signed equivalents of phonemes. If these considerations are compelling, refraining from ascribing to the *Tractatus* an additive conception of linguistic signs in the absence of compelling textual evidence to the contrary complies with the principles of exegetical charity.

3.6 Going Below the Linguistic Order?

Even if one is skeptical about the possibility of an account of linguistic signs that makes no reference to linguistic meaning, one might still wonder whether there is room for a theory of sense that goes below the level of linguistic signs. Every particular occurrence of a linguistic sign can be described in a conceptual apparatus that makes no reference to meaning and the order of language. The words one utters or writes down on a specific occasion can be specified, for instance, in purely acoustic or geometrical terms. One may wonder, therefore, whether a foothold for the application of a theory of sense could be gained by descending to this sublinguistic level of description. The input to be tested for nonsensicality would consist, for example, in arrangements of acoustic or geometrical repeatables – where two particulars count as occurrences of the same repeatable in so far as they vary within a range of approximation that is defined, once again, in purely acoustic or geometrical terms.

Exegetically, the difficulty with this proposal is that there is no explicit evidence that the *Tractatus* has an interest in considering language from this sublinguistic perspective. Moreover, it is disputable that Wittgenstein ever had such an interest, except when he was problematizing the idea that one can climb up to the linguistic level from a sublinguistic position (Bronzo 2017, Conant 2020b). Philosophically, the difficulty is that the prospects of a theory of sense

---

[45] For a classical discussion, see Jakobson (1978).

[46] See for instance Bromberger & Halle (1986). For additional discussion of the linguistics literature, see Conant (2020a, Section XIII).

applied to input specified in purely sublinguistic terms are very doubtful. If, as suggested in the previous section, there is in general no way of capturing the variation of linguistic signs in terms of sublinguistic variation, the theory of sense will have to legislate on the irredeemable nonsensicality of nonlinguistic structures without being able to specify to which linguistic signs they belong. Yet it is hard to see how this could be done in any remotely plausible way. On which basis could a theory maintain, for instance, that a certain acoustic or geometrical sequence is nonsensical, if it cannot even determine, say, whether it amounts to an occurrence of the sentence "Socrates is an object" or "Socrates is an abject"? Certainly, whether one speaks sense or nonsense depends on the words one utters.

3.7 Versions of the "Austere" Conception of Nonsense

The conception of language ascribed to the *Tractatus* in Sections 3.2–3.6 can be said to involve a commitment to a particularly strong version of the "austere" conception of nonsense. Cora Diamond and James Conant introduced the term to characterize a central tenet of their "resolute" reading of the *Tractatus*.[47] Over the years, they have stated that conception in various ways, including the following:

1) There is no such thing as a sentence that is nonsensical on account of the intelligible content it somehow manages to convey.[48]
2) There is no such thing as a sentence that is nonsensical on account of the meanings of its parts and manner of combination.[49]
2a) If a sentence is nonsensical, it contains at least one meaningless word. However, some of its words may be meaningful, and all of its words may belong to logicosyntactical categories.[50]

---

[47] See, for example, Diamond (2000, p. 153) and Conant (2000, pp. 176, 191). In earlier writings, Diamond referred to the "Frege-Wittgenstein conception of nonsense" (Diamond 1991, p. 96). I assume that the two pieces of terminology are equivalent.

[48] Diamond writes, for example, that according to Wittgenstein's "austere" conception of nonsense, to call something nonsensical is to imply "that it has really and truly got no articulable content" (Diamond 2000, p. 155). Similarly, Conant writes that the austere conception of nonsense rules out the idea of nonsense that "expresses a logically incoherent thought" (Conant 2000, p. 176).

[49] For Diamond, the "Frege-Wittgenstein view" holds that there is no "positive nonsense," i.e., "no kind of nonsense which is nonsense on account of what the terms composing it mean" (Diamond 1991, p. 106). For Conant, the austere conception of nonsense rules out "substantial nonsense," i.e., nonsense that "is composed of intelligible ingredients combined in an illegitimate way" (Conant 2000, p. 176). In the context of Conant's discussion of the *Tractatus*, the relevant ingredients are sentential components.

[50] "For Wittgenstein, a sentence is nonsensical if it contains a word or words to which no meaning has been given" (Diamond 2000, p. 163). This implies that not all the words of a nonsensical sentence must be meaningless. In the same essay, Diamond maintains that a nonsensical

2b) If a sentence is nonsensical, all of its words are meaningless. However, all of them may belong to logicosyntactical categories.[51]

2c) If a sentence is nonsensical, none of its words is meaningful, and none of them belongs to a logicosyntactical category.[52]

3) The nonsensicality of a sentence is always due to some absence of meaning, not to the presence of the wrong sort of meaning.[53]

There is a question about whether Diamond, Conant, or other resolute readers would regard any of these formulations – or some other one – as fundamental. Without trying to answer this question, we can notice the following.

The first formulation had priority in the dialectical context in which the resolute reading first developed. The main target of the approach was a sort of ineffabilist reading of the *Tractatus* that distinguished between (a) *mere nonsense*, which is simply unintelligible, and (b) the form of *deep nonsense* exemplified by the sentences of the *Tractatus*, which in spite of their nonsensicality somehow manage to convey insights into the nature of language, thought, and reality – where the insights in question would simply be *said* by the sentences that convey them if per impossible these sentences could count as senseful. Ascribing (1) to the *Tractatus* was meant to block this sort of ineffabilist reading.

Resolute readers have often treated (1) and (2) as equivalent.[54] However, some critics have denied that (1) entails (2), arguing that one may accept combinatorial nonsense while denying that it conveys any sort of intelligible content.[55] Regardless of how this controversy is to be adjudicated, there are certainly substantial differences between (2a), (2b), and (2c). As the numbering indicates, they are alternative specifications of (2). The difference concerns *how*

---

sentence, for the *Tractatus*, has logicosyntactical form: "A sentence that is meaningless is ... a symbol which has the general form of a proposition, and which fails to have sense simply because we have not given it any" (Diamond 2000, p. 151; see also Diamond 2011, p. 246).

[51] "On the Frege-Wittgenstein view, if a sentence makes no sense, no part of it can be said to mean what it does in some other sentence which does make sense" (Diamond 1991, p. 111). This passage rules out (2a) and leaves room for (2b) and (2c).

[52] Conant defines the austere conception of nonsense as the view for which the only possible kind of nonsense is "mere nonsense," understood as "a string composed of signs in which no symbol can be perceived, and which hence has no discernible logical syntax" (Conant 2000, p. 191).

[53] "*Anything* that is nonsense is so merely because some determination of meaning has *not* been made; it is not nonsense as a logical result of determinations that *have* been made" (Diamond 1991, p. 106).

[54] At one point, for instance, Conant treats the idea excluded by (1) as a mere gloss on the idea excluded by (2): "Substantial nonsense is composed of intelligible ingredients combined in an illegitimate way – it expresses a logically incoherent thought" (Conant 2000, p. 176).

[55] See, for example, Schönbaumsfeld (2007, pp. 106–108). It should be noticed that resolute readers, at least on some occasions, do not simply assume that (1) entails (2), but argue for it. See Diamond (1991, pp. 104–105) and Goldfarb (1997, p. 59).

much a nonsensical sentence can have in common with a meaningful sentence – or, equivalently, how much a failed exercise of our capacity to use language to make sense can have in common with its successful exercise. As we progress from (2a) to (2c), the posited common factor is increasingly restricted. For (2a), a failure to make sense involves also *some* failure of our capacity to express subsentential contents; for (2b), it involves a *complete* failure of such a capacity; for (2c), it also involves a failure of our capacity to produce linguistic signs having logicosyntactical form. Each of these versions of (2) entails (3). They all imply that the nonsensicality of a sentence is always due to some absence or privation of meaning. The difference concerns the minimal unit of privation that can be responsible for the nonsensicality of a sentence. Suppose that we define the "strength" of a version of (2) so as to make it inversely proportional to the extent of the common factor between a meaningful and a nonsensical sentence that it condones – or, equivalently, directly proportional to the extent of the minimal unit of privation that it takes to be responsible for the nonsensicality of a sentence. On this definition, the progression from (2a) to (2c) takes us from a comparatively *weak* to an increasingly *stronger* version of (2).

The reading of the Tractarian conception of language presented in Sections 3.2–3.6 follows (2c) in denying that there is any semantic or logico-syntactical common factor between sense and nonsense. But it goes beyond (2c) in holding explicitly that the *Tractatus* does not take linguistic signs to constitute an independently intelligible common factor between sense and nonsense. On the nonadditive account outlined above, to succeed in producing linguistic signs when one utters nonsense consists simply in *failing* to produce symbols – that is, in failing to make sense. To say that someone who utters nonsense produces linguistic signs is a way of characterizing a failure, not a success. When one fails to make sense, there is no layer of the linguistic performance that remains unaffected by the failure. Thus, if we take a commitment to (2) to be a sufficient condition for qualifying as an "austere" conception of nonsense, and if we measure the "strength" of a version of such a conception in the way described above, then we can say that the view of language ascribed to the *Tractatus* in the previous sections involves a very strong version of the austere conception of nonsense.

3.8 Nonsense, the Logic/Psychology Dichotomy, and Linguistic Intentions

The notion of a *failed exercise of a capacity*, which figures prominently in the account of the Tractarian conception of language given in Sections 3.2–3.6, helps to avoid problems raised by a feature of some common presentations of the austere conception of nonsense – namely, the appeal to a Frege-inspired distinction between logic and psychology.

As we have seen, the austere conception of nonsense, on one of its formulations, holds that nonsense is always due to some absence of meaning, rather than to the presence of a wrong sort of meaning (Section 3.7). To use an example discussed by Diamond, if the sentence "Caesar is a prime number" is nonsensical, it is nonsensical *for the same sort of reason* for which "Scott kept a runcible at Abbotsford" is nonsensical. Appearances notwithstanding, the former sentence contains one or more words that are, in that context, as meaningless as "runcible" (Diamond 1991, p. 102; for similar examples, see pp. 107 and 197). If nonsense is always due to an absence of meaning, there is in this sense only one kind of nonsense. Yet, one may distinguish between different kinds of nonsense on other grounds. It is at this juncture that resolute readers have often appealed to a distinction between logic and psychology explicitly derived from Frege. Nonsense is always due to a lack of *logical* meaning, and in this sense, there is "logically" only one kind of nonsense (Diamond 1991, p. 102; Conant 2000, p. 191). However, one may distinguish between kinds of nonsense in other ways, and one way of doing so is to consider the "psychological accompaniments" of words (Diamond 1991, pp. 97–103).

The relevant notion of psychological accompaniment is derived mainly from a passage of *The Foundations of Arithmetic* where Frege comments on the connection between the principle of the separation of logic and psychology ("Always to separate sharply the psychological from the logical, the subjective from the objective") and the Context Principle ("Never to ask for the meaning of a word in isolation, but always in the context of a proposition"). Frege remarks that "if the second principle is not observed, one is almost forced to take as the meanings of words mental pictures or acts of the individual mind, and so to offend against the first principle as well" (Frege 1980, p. xxii). Frege's reserves the term "ideas" for the "mental pictures or acts of the individual mind" that may accompany the use of words, and employs the term "meaning" in a logical sense, to designate the contribution that a word makes to the truth-conditions of the sentence in which it occurs. A central point of the distinction is that a word may be associated with the same ideas even when it has different logical meanings, or no logical meaning at all, as when it occurs in isolation. For example, as Frege observes later on in the same book (§51), the word "moon" is used sometimes as a proper name ("The Moon is a satellite") and sometimes as a concept-word ("Jupiter has four moons"). On these two sorts of occurrence, the word has different logical meanings – indeed, categorically different ones – but it may be accompanied by the same ideas. For instance, it may give rise to the same mental picture of a whitish disk on a dark background. The same may happen when the word does not occur as a logically working part of a meaningful sentence.

Drawing on this Fregean distinction between logical meanings and psychological ideas, resolute readers have often maintained that one of the differences between "Caesar is a prime number" and "Scott kept a runcible at Abbotsford" is that the latter, unlike the former, contains a word that is not associated to ideas accompanying its logical use, since there is no established way of putting it to logical use. In this sense, the word lacks psychological accompaniments. At this point, resolute readers have tended to subsume indistinctly under the category of "psychological accompaniment" both mental pictures and intentions to use words with certain logical meanings (Diamond 1991, pp. 98–99, 103; Diamond 2000, p. 159; Conant 2000, p. 190). This move might be faithful to Frege, since Fregean "ideas," as we saw, include both "mental pictures" and "acts of the individual mind." However, the move itself is problematic, because it tends to obscure the relevance of linguistic intentions for a proper characterization of nonsense as a failure to make sense.

There is an important difference between mental pictures and linguistic intentions. If I intend to use a word with a certain logical meaning, and the word turns out to lack that meaning, I thereby *fail* to use the word with that meaning. By contrast, if I utter a word and entertain the mental picture that normally accompanies a certain logical employment of the word, and I do not put the word to that logical use, I do *not* thereby fail to give the word that logical meaning, since I might not even be trying to do so. I might be simply uttering the word in order to observe and savor its associated mental pictures – uttering the word, in one of Wittgenstein's beautiful images, as "striking a note on the keyboard of the imagination" (PI §6).

The problem is that entertaining mental pictures while uttering words on the one hand, and putting words to logical use on the other, are two achievements in their own right with separate conditions of success. They may be empirically connected, but the lack of the connection on any particular occasion does not show that there has been a failure with respect to either achievement. Thus, assimilating linguistic intentions to mental pictures deprives us of the resources for characterizing nonsense as a failure to make sense and for distinguishing it from employments of language that may be sensibly called "nonsensical," but do not involve any failure to make sense (Section 1.1). When one utters "Scott kept a runcible at Abbotsford" with no intention of stipulating a new meaning for the word "runcible," one is not failing to make sense, because one is not even trying to do so. One may be said to speak "nonsense," but not in the sense of failing to make sense. By contrast, if one utters "Caesar is a prime number," intending to use "Caesar" as it is employed in "Caesar crossed the Rubicon," and "is a prime number" as it is employed in "2 is a prime number," and intending to predicate the property expressed by the latter expression of the person designated by the former, one is indeed trying to make sense, and if the sentence lacks sense, one is failing to do so. This difference becomes invisible if linguistic intentions are construed on the model of mental pictures.

I suggest that the assimilation of linguistic intentions to mental pictures is at the root of the dissatisfaction that critics of resolute readings have often voiced against accounts of the difference between kinds of nonsense in terms of psychological accompaniments. The appeal to the presence or absence of associated mental pictures has been widely perceived as *irrelevant* for an account of the difference between the nonsensicality of "Caesar is a prime number" and the nonsensicality of "Scott kept a runcible at Abbottsford." The explanation offered by critics of resolute readings has typically involved a commitment to the possibility of combinatorial nonsense, and thus a rejection of the view that nonsense is always due to the absence of meaning (Glock 2004). Yet one may agree with such critics that a proper characterization of nonsense as a failure to make sense must involve a reference to the logical employment of linguistic expressions, while also retaining the idea that nonsense is always a matter of absence of logical meaning.

The notion of linguistic intention is fit for the task. In order to construe the utterance of "Caesar is a prime number" as a failure to make sense, we need to hold that the speaker intends to assign its component expressions determinate logical meanings and combine them in a logically determinate way. However, we do not need to hold that all of these intentions are fulfilled, as the advocate of combinatorial nonsense has it. On the contrary, we can maintain that at least some of the relevant intentions are frustrated, and this is enough to adhere to the view that nonsense is always due to some absence of logical meaning.[56]

On the strong version of the austere conception of nonsense ascribed above to the *Tractatus* (Section 3.2–3.6), a failure to make sense entails the frustration of *all* the linguistic intentions involved in the performance: the intention to express some intelligible sentential content; the intention to use words with actual subsentential meanings; and the intention to use words belonging, in actuality, to logicosyntactical categories. When one fails to make sense, one does indeed

---

[56] It would be psychologistic, by both Fregean and Tractarian lights, to hold that linguistic intentions fix the logical role that a word is actually playing on a given occasion, but the present proposal is not guilty of this form of psychologism. Linguistic intentions fix only the meaning that the speaker is *trying* to give to a word on a given occasion, not whether they *succeed* in doing so. Compare Moore (2003, p. 187) and Sullivan (2003, pp. 212–214).

produce signs, but this is not the fulfillment of a separate intention, but the *frustration* of the intention to produce symbols.

Linguistic intentions, on this conception, are present in both the successful and the failed exercise of the capacity for the significant employment of language. But this does not entail that the capacity to use language to make sense is factorized into a subcapacity to have linguistic intentions which can be successfully exercised even when the more encompassing capacity is not. One can maintain, in fact, that there is no separate capacity to have linguistic intentions. Rather, to have linguistic intentions – either fulfilled or frustrated – consists simply in exercising the fallible, self-conscious capacity to use language to make sense. To have a fulfilled linguistic intention is to exercise this capacity successfully, and to have a frustrated linguistic intention is to exercise it unsuccessfully.[57]

4 Clarification Without a Theory of Sense

4.1 Presenting Possibilities of Sense

If Wittgenstein rejected the idea of a theory of sense, in which way is his philosophy meant to unmask illusions of sense? And more specifically, if the rules of logical syntax (in his early writings) or grammar (in his later writings) are not meant to serve as nonsensicality tests, what is their role in uncovering failures to make sense? The rest of this Element discusses a way of answering these questions that generalizes ideas presented by resolute readers in connection with their interpretation of the Tractarian conception of the role of an adequate notation, or adequate *Zeichensprache* (TLP 3.325), in philosophical clarification.[58]

Resolute readers such as Cora Diamond (1991, pp. 115–144) and James Conant (2002, pp. 411–414) have opposed the following understanding of how a notation can be used for the *Tractatus* to reveal the nonsensicality of apparently meaningful sentences. One translates the problematic sentences into formulae of an adequate notation – in a manner that preserves the logical categories and mode of combination of the components of the original sentences – and then checks whether the formulae comply with the rules of the notation. If the formulae violate the syntactical rules of the notation, the corresponding sentences of natural language are nonsensical, because they involve an illegitimate combination of

---

[57] For an insightful discussion of issues that are structurally similar to those examined in this section, see Nunez (2019).

[58] The Tractarian term "*Zeichensprache*," literally a "sign-language," can be paraphrased as "a system of signs for the expression of thoughts." The *Tractatus* mentions the conceptual notation or *Begriffsschrift* "of Frege and Russell" as an example of a *Zeichensprache* that is more adequate than ordinary language for the purpose of avoiding illusions of sense (TLP 3.325). The *Tractatus* is evidently focusing on the structural similarities between Frege's and Russell's respective notations. Its judgment about their greater adequacy would extend to standard contemporary logical notation, which shares many of those structural features.

logicosyntactical categories. The *Tractatus*, for instance, implies that "A is an object" is nonsensical (where "A" purports to be a name and "object" purports to express a logical category).[59] On the reading opposed by Diamond and Conant, one could demonstrate the nonsensicality of the sentence by translating it into an ill-formed formula of contemporary logical notation, say "$\exists x(A)$." The counter-syntactical character of the formula is supposed to show that the original sentence combines expressions belonging to the wrong logical categories.[60]

By contrast, Diamond and Conant have argued that for the *Tractatus* there is no such thing as a translation of a nonsensical sentence into an adequate logical notation (Conant & Diamond 2004, pp. 57–58). A nonsensical sentence is precisely a sentence that *lacks* any such translation. An adequate notation can serve as a tool for revealing illusions of sense by clearly presenting different possibilities of sense – different ways of putting signs to significant use. The adequacy of a notation for this purpose is determined by the extent to which it makes categorically different employments of signs clearly distinguishable. Illusions of sense derive from the fact that we are unclear about how we want to employ our signs, and a good notation, by making different uses clearly distinguishable, can help us to realize that we need to make up our minds.

Let's illustrate the view by considering again "A is an object."[61] It will help, first, to have in sight more details about the Tractarian treatment of this sort of example. Wittgenstein points out that there is a common use of the word "object" as a term for a "formal concept" that is rendered in a perspicuous logical notation by means of a variable (TLP 4.1272). For instance, the sentence "There are objects which are books," understood as a roundabout way of saying that there are books, is rendered in standard contemporary logical notation as "$\exists x(Bx)$." Wittgenstein contrasts terms for formal concepts with proper concept-words, which ascribe genuine properties and are rendered in the same notation by means of functional expressions. The sentence "A is a book," for instance, translates as "B(A)." The *Tractatus* contends that "wherever [the word 'object'] is used otherwise, i.e. as a proper concept-word, there arise nonsensical pseudo-propositions" (TLP 4.1272). It gives as examples "There are objects" and "There are 100 objects," and it is clear that it would consider "A is an object" as an equally good example.

---

[59] See TLP 4.1272. I will say more shortly about the Tractarian understanding of this sort of example.

[60] Compare Williams (2004, p. 15): "Philosophical 'object' talk is [for the *Tractatus*] really a way of introducing existential quantification. A perspicuous analysis of the sentence ['A is an object'] reveals this transparently: '(Ex)A' is transparent nonsense." Conant and Diamond (2004, pp. 57–58) take Williams' discussion to exemplify the view they oppose.

[61] The following account draws on Conant & Diamond (2004, pp. 57–58).

On the reading proposed by Diamond and Conant, the *Tractatus* holds that these sentences are nonsensical, as we typically use them in philosophy, because they express unclarity on our part about how we want to use the word "object" – and specifically, an unresolved wavering between (a) a desire to use it as a proper concept-word such as "book," and (b) a desire to use it as a term for a formal concept. We *could* use "object" as a genuine concept-word, but then we would need to decide *which* property we want to ascribe by means of it. (We could naturally mean, for instance, the property of being medium-size and solid by human standards, as when one says that that the room is filled with objects.) The problem with the aforementioned sentences, as they typically occur in philosophy, is that we do not think that there is any need to make this determination of meaning, because we simply want to use the word "object" with the meaning it already has when it is used as a term for a formal concept in sentences such as "There are objects which are books." We want to use it *that* way, while also using it as "book" in "A is a book," that is, to ascribe a property to something. The formulae of an adequate notation can help to see that *there is no such thing as doing that*. When we want to say, in a philosophical mood, "A is an object," we can ask ourselves: Do we want to use the word "object" so that the whole sentence would go over in the notation as "O(A)"? In that case, we need to decide which property we want to express by means of the functional-expression "O(. . .)." Or do we want to use the word "object" so that it would go over in the notation as a variable, as in the formula "$\exists x(Bx)$"? But in that case, the word "object" is not used at all to ascribe a property, and the rest of the sentence must be used in a way that differs completely (in both meaning and form) from the way it is used in "A is a book."

We can do either thing – use "object" as a proper concept-word, or use it as a term for a formal concept – making in each case the appropriate adjustments. What an adequate notation can help us to see is that *we need to make up our minds*. For while we can go either way, there is no such thing as somehow going both ways at once. An adequate notation, on this reading, can be described as a tool for interrogating our relation to our words (cf. Goldfarb 1997, p. 71). One can also say that it is a tool of self-knowledge, in so far as it helps to become aware of unclarities about what we want to do with our words.

This account of the use of an adequate notation for revealing illusions of sense can be used as a model for a more general understanding of Wittgenstein's conception of philosophical clarification, in the *Tractatus* as well as in the later works. Diamond's recent discussion and critique of "exclusionary" readings of the *Tractatus* goes in this direction (Diamond 2019, especially pp. 126–127). For Diamond, the *Tractatus* does not aim to propose a theory of the significant use of language that excludes other uses of language as nonsensical. In particular, it does not aim to put forth a picture theory of the proposition that rules out nonpicturing uses as nonsensical. Instead, it simply aims to lay out the picturing use of language and a variety of other uses (such as the use of tautologies, mathematical equations, rules of translation, fundamental laws of physics, identity statements, and probability propositions) in a manner that makes their differences – and the commitments that accompany each kind of use – clearly visible. The point of this exercise is to make us aware of cases in which we have no clear conception of what we want to do with language, but hover confusedly between different options. As Diamond puts it, "no use of words is excluded by laying out a use of words; but laying out a use of words can be meant to sharpen our eyes to the fact that a supposed way of using words is not anything at all" (p. 127). More specifically, presenting clearly the picturing use of language and how it differs from a variety of nonpicturing uses is supposed to help to identify cases in which we dither indeterminately between wanting to use our words in a picturing and nonpicturing way:

> The laying out of [the picturing use of signs] doesn't exclude any other use of signs, but it does help to bring out a certain kind of confusion, in which one is at one and the same time using, or apparently attempting to use, signs in such a way, and also not using them in that way . . . What is excluded by laying out the picture-proposition use is a kind of unconscious slipperiness, in which you take for granted the picture-proposition use and its abrogation at the same time. (Diamond 2019, p. 126)

There is a question about how much of the *Tractatus* can be seen as presenting uses of language in this sense. Diamond maintains that by Tractarian lights a use of language is presented by "specifying the values of a propositional variable" and rejects the view that the elucidatory propositions of the *Tractatus* (namely, those that according to TLP 6.54 must be eventually recognized as nonsensical) serve to describe the use or grammar of linguistic expressions and are in this respect akin to the grammatical propositions of later Wittgenstein (Diamond 2019, pp. 123–124, in response to Moyal-Sharrock 2007). However, this seems to me a point where one can disagree with Diamond, even if one accepts her central contention about the nonexclusionary character of the Tractarian conception of clarification.

In this connection, I would like to make the following suggestions. First, most of what happens in the *Tractatus* consists in fact in the presentation of uses of language – including, most prominently, the set of elucidatory propositions that articulate the so-called picture theory of the proposition. After all, where should we look for the presentation of the picturing use of language, if not in the sentences that ostensibly describe what it is for language to picture reality?

Secondly, if the idea that the propositions of the *Tractatus* serve to present uses of language turned out to be hard to square with the injunction to throw away the ladder (TLP 6.54), one should question the soundness of that injunction – not because it relies on an overly restrictive theory of what can count as making sense, but because it expresses a mistaken attempt to clarify the sort of clarificatory use of language exemplified by the *Tractatus* (see Section 1.7). Thirdly, a great deal of what happens in Wittgenstein's later works can also be seen as the presentation of uses of language, including not only the employment of grammatical propositions, but also the formulation of logicosyntactical/grammatical rules, which takes a prominent role in the writings of the early Thirties. Stating the rules for the use of linguistic expressions can serve to present ways of making sense and make us aware that sometimes we are simultaneously willing and not willing to use an expression according to a given set of rules, and thus simultaneously willing and not willing to use it in a particular way, and thus failing to put it to any determinate use.

4.2 Violating the Rules of Logical Syntax/Grammar

Some resolute readers have argued that for the *Tractatus* there is no such thing as a violation of logicosyntactical rules, while critics have challenged this contention on both exegetical and philosophical grounds.[62] I want to argue that the nonfactorizing conception of language ascribed to Wittgenstein in Section 3 – which develops and radicalizes ideas characteristically advanced by resolute readers – is compatible with a relevant sense in which nonsense arises from a violation of logicosyntactical/grammatical rules. However, I will leave largely open how the following proposal relates to the dispute between resolute readers and their critics. Identifying the exact claims and arguments of each side of that dispute – and thus, what exactly the dispute is about – is a complex task of its own, going beyond the scope of this Element.

There is considerable exegetical pressure to make room for some construal of the idea that logicosyntactical/grammatical rules can be violated, and that when this happens, the result is nonsense. Admittedly, neither the *Tractatus* nor the *Investigations* speak explicitly of such "violations" or "transgressions," but they do speak of "rules" of logical syntax/grammar (Sections 1.3 and 1.5), and it is hard to see what is left of the concept of a rule if we take away the very possibility of acting in a way that goes against the rule. Moreover, the *Tractatus* comes very close to speaking of violations of rules of logical syntax

---

[62] See especially the exchange between Conant (2001) and Hacker (2000b, pp. 365–367; 2003), followed by defenses of Conant's approach in Diamond (2005) and Gustafsson (2020). See also Moore (2003, p. 186), Sullivan (2003, p. 208), and Engelmann (2011).

when it says that "[w]herever the word 'object' ... is correctly used [*richtig gebraucht*], it is expressed in logical symbolism by the variable," but "[w]henever it used otherwise, i.e. as a proper concept-word, there arise non-sensical pseudo-propositions" (TLP 4.1272). This suggests that nonsensical pseudo-propositions result from an *incorrect* use of words. Similarly, commenting on the English translation of TLP 3.326, Wittgenstein glosses the expression "significant use" as use "in accordance with the laws of logical syntax" or "syntactically correct" use (LO p. 59). Once again, it is not clear how a use can be syntactically correct if it cannot be syntactically incorrect. In the writings of the late 1920s and early 1930s, the idea that nonsense involves a violation of logicosyntactical/grammatical rules becomes more prominent and explicit. For instance, Wittgenstein characterizes the rules of logical syntax as "the rules which tell us in which connections only a word gives sense, thus excluding nonsensical structures" (RLF 129); he traces the nonsensicality of a sentence to the "misuse" of words ("it's nonsense to say that I am safe *whatever* happens ... this is a misuse of the word 'safe,'" LE 9); and he writes that "the rules of grammar determine ... whether a combination of words has sense or not" (BT 63/79).[63]

As a preliminary to interpreting these passages, let's say that a capacity can have *external* or *internal conditions*, to be distinguished as follows: a condition is external, if its satisfaction is not required for the successful exercise of the capacity; and it is internal, if its satisfaction is required for the successful exercise of the capacity. Let's also say that a rule is *constitutive* of a given capacity if it specifies internal conditions of the capacity, and *nonconstitutive* otherwise. A familiar pair of examples will illustrate the distinction. Take driving and driving according to the traffic regulations of a certain area. At least according to a familiar notion of driving, traffic regulations lay down merely external conditions on driving: one's driving can be fully successful, qua driving, even if it violates traffic regulations. By contrast, let's take playing chess and playing according to the rules of chess. The rules of chess specify internal conditions of playing chess: a move will be defective, qua chess move, if it does not comply with the chess rules. The rules of chess are constitutive of chess, while particular sets of traffic regulations are nonconstitutive of driving.

The rules of logical syntax/grammar, being rules, specify conditions; and being the rules that they are, specify conditions for making sense. On the nonfactorizing conception of language ascribed to Wittgenstein in Section 3, the rules of logical syntax/grammar cannot specify conditions that are *external*

---

[63] For additional textual evidence, see Hacker (2003, pp. 12–14). Diamond (2005) contests the putative evidence from the *Tractatus*.

to any part or aspect of the capacity to use language to make sense.[64] This is so because, on that conception, our linguistic capacity is unified in such a manner that a failure to make sense affects the entirety of the linguistic order. When one fails to use language to make sense, one also fails to express subsentential meanings and to produce signs belonging to logicosyntactical categories (Sections 3.2–3.4). One does indeed produce linguistic signs, but this is not the successful exercise of a self-standing capacity, since to produce linguistic signs when one fails to make sense consists simply in failing to make sense (Section 3.5). There is therefore no such thing as a violation of the rules of logical syntax/grammar, if these rules are taken to specify conditions that are external to the successful exercise of any part or aspect of the capacity to use language to make sense.

However, the rules of logical syntax/grammar can be taken to specify internal conditions of our nonfactorizable capacity for the significant use of language – and thus, conditions that are constitutive of any part or aspect of its exercise. On this view, to specify the logicosyntactical/grammatical rules for the use of an expression is to present a way of using it to make sense, and to violate these rules is to *fail* to give the expression the sort of significant use that the rules contribute to constitute, in a manner that affects the entirety of the linguistic order.

Let's illustrate the point by applying it to the account of the nonsensicality of "A is an object" given in the previous section. To say that the word "object" works as a term for a formal concept and that "A is an object" *violates* the logicosyntactical rules governing its employment is a way of saying that it involves a failure to use it as a term for a formal concept – a failure to put it to the sort of significant use that those logicosyntactical rules contribute to constitute. One *wants* to use it in accordance with the rules that contribute to constitute its use as a term for a formal concept. However, one *also* wants to use it in accordance with the rules that contribute to constitute the use of genuine concept-words, without realizing that these are very different rules, constituting a different use and carrying different commitments. As a result of this unwitting wavering between different sets of rules and the corresponding uses they contribute to constitute, one fails to put the word to any significant use at all. The word has in this context no content and no logicosyntactical form, and its very identity as a word is given by its failure to be a significant sign.

---

[64] Here and below, the "parts or aspects" of the capacity to use language to make sense should be understood as belonging to the linguistic order. Thus, they do not include capacities that may be required for the significant use of language, but whose description does not necessarily involve linguistic notions (such as, for instance, the capacity to move one's lips and tongue).

When one fails to follow logicosyntactical/grammatical rules in this manner, the rules continue to *bear* on the linguistic performance. The speaker *purports* to follow certain rules but does not do so. In this sense, they *violate* the rules. It is essential that the rules bear in this manner on the performance, because this is what makes of the performance a *failure*, rather than an instance of successfully doing something else. There is a crucial difference between (a) purporting to follow the constitutive rules of Φ-ing without actually doing so, and (b) not following the constitutive rules of Φ-ing because one purports to follow the constitutive rules of some other activity. Only in the former case one fails to Φ.[65]

A theory of sense, as defined in Section 2.1, is essentially committed to specifying conditions that are *external* to the linguistic performances that it tests for nonsensicality, for only in that way can it provide a test in which the input is independent of the results. This does not mean, however, that the difference between a theory of sense on the one hand, and the nonfactorizing conception of language I ascribed to Wittgenstein on the other, lies merely in the fact that the latter conceives of logicosyntactical/grammatical rules as *constitutive* of making sense and of the conditions they specify as *internal* to making sense. Theories of sense may very well share this commitment. A theory of sense may hold that purporting to satisfy the conditions it specifies without actually doing so results in a *failure to make sense*, and thus in *not making sense at all*, as opposed to successfully making sense in a manner that fails to satisfy a further set of merely external conditions. Hence, a theory of sense is not necessarily committed to the paradoxical idea that nonsense consists in making a wrong or illegitimate sort of sense (cf. Hacker 2000b, pp. 366–367). But even when a theory of sense construes the conditions it specifies as internal to the capacity for the significant use of language, *it reduces them to external conditions of some linguistic subcapacity* – such as the capacity to combine meaningful words, or logicosyntactical items, or mere signs conceived as specifiable without any reference to their significant use. By contrast, the nonfactorizing conception of language that I ascribed to Wittgenstein rejects this sort of reduction. The internal conditions of the capacity for the significant use of language are at the same time internal conditions of any part or aspect of that capacity. A failure to satisfy those conditions affects, accordingly, all descriptions of the linguistic performance that remain within the linguistic order.[66]

---

[65] Hence, as already argued in Section 3.8, linguistic intentions are essential to a characterization of nonsense as a failure to make sense.

[66] If one wishes, one may employ the label "theory of sense" to refer to the specification of internal conditions of the nonfactorizable capacity for the significant use of language. The only thing that matters for the purposes in this Element is that this way of employing the terminology differs from the one I introduced. I am only invested in the distinction that I introduced by means of that terminology, not in the terminology in itself.

As mentioned above, some resolute readers have opposed the very idea that nonsense arises from a violation of logicosyntactical/grammatical rules. In some cases, the opposition appears to be motivated by the claim that the nonsensicality of a use of language cannot be inferred from the mere fact that it deviates from some established set of rules (Diamond 2005), but this is a questionable motivation. On the proposal I have presented, a failure to make sense can indeed be described as a violation of logicosyntactical/grammatical rules (in so far as these rules are construed as constitutive of the nonfactorizable capacity for the significant use of language), but deviation from established rules does not entail any failure to make sense. This is due to the essential role of linguistic intentions. In order to fail to follow a set of rules, one must intend to follow them. Thus, if a person is not using a word in accordance with any preexistent set of rules, it does not follow that they are not making sense, for they may intend to use the word in accordance with some unprecedented set of rules, and succeed in doing so.[67]

I have argued that a nonfactorizing conception of language is compatible with the claim that nonsense arises from a violation of logicosyntactical/grammatical rules. The whole argument has been premised on the assumption that specifying logicosyntactical/grammatical rules is an appropriate way of presenting significant uses of language. For the Wittgenstein of the *Investigations*, this assumption is valid only to a limited extent. While the *Investigations* mentions at one point "rules of grammar" (PI §497), the notion does not play the central role it had in the writings of the early thirties. In fact, the explicit methodological pluralism of the *Investigations* (PI §133) opposes the idea that "tabulating rules" for the use of expressions is a universal weapon against philosophical confusions, as Wittgenstein maintained in the early thirties (WVC 184). Moreover, in the *Investigations* Wittgenstein attacks the view that using an expression to make sense consists in following a sharply defined set of rules. He explicitly denies that "if anyone utters a sentence and *means* or *understands* it he is operating a calculus according to definite rules" (PI §81). He holds that sharply defined systems of rules can help to clarify the use of language when employed as "objects of comparison," as opposed to accounts of what significant uses of language must amount to (PI §81, §130). And his discussion of "family resemblances" (PI §§66–67) undermines the idea that the unity of a use of language is generally given by a fixed set of rules.

From the perspective of the *Investigations*, there are therefore important limitations to the view that uses of language can be presented by stating

---

[67] New significant uses of language need not share the arbitrariness of Humpty Dumpty's. They may be immediately intelligible to masters of the language. For an influential discussion, see Cavell (1999, pp. 168–190).

logicosyntactical/grammatical rules. What I have argued for in this section remains relevant for the interpretation of the *Investigations* in the following respect: one may coherently reject theories of sense and yet refer to nonsense as a *misuse* of language and a *violation* of grammar. These phrases can be understood as ways of characterizing failures to meet the internal conditions of our nonfactorizable capacity for the significant use of language, even though these internal conditions cannot be captured by static and sharply delimited sets of rules.

4.3 Clarification and Collective Self-knowledge

On the present approach, a failure to make sense is not a linguistic performance that does not satisfy some external condition specified by a theory of sense. It is instead the expression of a confusion. When we fail to make sense, we do not really know what we want to do with our words. Recognizing a failure to make sense marks therefore progress in self-knowledge. The central goal of Wittgenstein's philosophy is, accordingly, to give us tools and technique of self-knowledge.

This progress in self-knowledge involves an essentially first-personal dimension. Philosophy can clearly lay out different significant uses of language; but it is up to each of us to connect these different possibilities to our own attempts to make sense, and to recognize what we are attempting to do as an actualization of one of those possibilities, or of some other possibility, or as a failure to make up our mind about which possibility we want to actualize. James Conant is among the commentators who have emphasized this point:

> Wittgenstein (both early and late) seeks a method that ultimately can only be practiced by someone on himself. Wittgenstein's method only permits the verdict that sense has not been spoken to be passed by the one who speaks. The role of a philosophical elucidator is not to pass verdicts on the statements of others, but to help them achieve clarity about what it is that they want to say. Thus the conversation does not break off if the other cannot meet the demand to make himself intelligible to the practitioner of philosophical elucidation; rather the burden lies with the one who professes to elucidate – not to specify a priori conditions of intelligibility, but rather to find the liberating word: enabling the other to attain intelligibility, where this may require helping him first to discover that he is unintelligible to himself.
>
> (Conant 2001, p. 61)

This passage connects the first-personal character of philosophical clarification (its being a "method that ultimately can only be practiced by someone on himself") to a certain form of response-dependency of any attempt to show that what somebody else is saying is nonsensical (the fact that "the conversation does not break off" until the self-professed elucidator succeeds in "enabling the other to attain intelligibility"). In a well-known passage comparing philosophy to psychoanalysis, Wittgenstein appears to insist on this response-dependency:

> One of the most important tasks is to express all false thought processes so true to character that the reader says, "Yes, that's exactly the way I meant it." To make a tracing of the physiognomy of every error.
>
> Indeed, we can only prove that someone made a mistake if he (really) acknowledges this expression as the correct expression of his feeling.
>
> For only if he acknowledges it as such, *is* it the correct expression. (Psychoanalysis.)
>
> What the other person acknowledges is the analogy I'm presenting to him as the source of his thought. (BT 303/410)

Wittgenstein seeks to trace philosophical confusions to misleading linguistic analogies; and the diagnosis is correct, *only if* the victim of the confusion – the "patient" – acknowledges it as such.

Yet, formulations of this sort, when taken in isolation, can lead to a distorted picture of the character of the response-dependency of philosophical clarification. The danger is to give undisputable authority to the actual response of the other person, making any attempt to identify and denounce nonsense hostage to the shortcomings of whomever we happen to be talking to. In order to attain an accurate picture of Wittgenstein's conception of the relevant response-dependency, we need to see how the previous sort of passage fits together with passages of this other sort:

> Language has the same traps ready for everyone; the immense network of easily trodden false paths. And thus we see one person after another walking down the same paths and we already know where he will make a turn, where he will keep going straight ahead without noticing the turn, etc., etc. Therefore wherever false paths branch off I ought to put up signs to help in getting past the dangerous spots. (BT 312/423)

The confusions that philosophical clarification addresses derive from misleading analogies that are built into our common language. Language is a shared capacity. In the terminology of the *Investigations*, it is a "practice" (PI §202), an assemblage of "customs (uses, institutions)" (PI §199). Illusions of sense are failed exercise of this shared capacity. When one fails to make sense, one falls into a trap that awaits anyone who speaks the same common language or a structurally similar language.

The truth in the idea that philosophical clarification is response-dependent is that the source of authority grounding any charge of nonsensicality is the same as the source of authority grounding the possible resistance to the charge – namely, the mastery of the language shared by the charger and the charged. This does not mean that one cannot be justified, and indeed be right, in thinking that what somebody is saying is nonsensical even if the other person happens to resist the allegation. But it means that the resources one mobilizes for identifying someone else's failure to make sense are always available to the other person, for they consist in the shared linguistic capacity that the other person exercises (defectively) in the very act of failing to make sense.

There is a contrast here between the present approach and the view that bases the critique of nonsense on the appeal to a theory of sense. For the latter, the grounds of the criticism are external to the linguistic capacities one exercises in failing to make sense. In relation to these capacities, the verdicts of theories of sense come as an alien piece of information. The factorization of our linguistic capacity posited by theories of sense is at the same time a factorization of our linguistic self. The part of ourselves that knows how to produce the linguistic input to be tested by the theory of sense does not have *in itself* the knowledge to reach those verdicts. The knowledge can only reside in a separate part of ourselves – a part that may in principle be more or less developed, or even altogether absent. Hence, this same knowledge can be imparted by someone *else*: some "guardian of sense" who can claim special expertise in the matters of sense, and on the basis of that expertise, simply *inform* us that, unfortunately, what we are saying makes no sense.

By contrast, on the nonfactorizing conception of language and the attending nonfactorizing conception of the linguistic self, the knowledge of what makes sense is already involved in the knowledge we exercise in any linguistic performance, even if defective. In order to become aware of a failure to make sense, we need to draw on the very capacity that we are defectively exercising: we need to come to see more clearly what we inevitably already know in virtue of the very fact that we are involved in such a failure. Wittgenstein's adaptation of the ancient doctrine that knowledge is recollection ("The work of the philosopher consists in assembling reminders for a particular purpose," PI §127; see also PI §§89, 90, 109 and BT 309/421) can be seen as an elaboration of this point. Theories of sense, from this perspective, presuppose an alienated relationship to what is in fact an inseparable dimension of who we are as masters of language.

Since failures to make sense are defective exercises of our shared linguistic capacity, the gain in self-knowledge obtained by becoming aware of any such failure is at the same time a gain in our *collective* self-knowledge: the knowledge of who *we* are – and of what we want, or fail to coherently want – as masters of a common language. My failure to make sense, along with my eventual recognition and overcoming of this failure, are never merely *mine*: they are live possibilities for whoever shares my language. When I struggle with my confusions, I act as representative of whoever bears the same linguistic capacity. At the same time, when I address the failures to make sense that happen to be voiced by another person, the failures are never merely *theirs*, but are live possibilities for whoever speaks their language, including myself. In philosophical clarification, the "I" and the "other" are subsumed under common heading of the "we."[68]

4.4 Defending the Contrast

In the post-introductory part of this Element, I have sought to draw a contrast between conceptions of philosophical clarification that rely on a theory of sense and conceptions that do not. My presentation of the exegetical debate, as well as my own claims about Wittgenstein, were framed in terms of this contrast. Now I want to address an objection that, if correct, would jeopardize the whole enterprise. The objection is that the contrast does not withstand closer examination, because the view I ascribed to Wittgenstein *is itself*, or at least *leaves room for*, a theory of sense.[69]

There are two features of the view I ascribed to Wittgenstein that may invite this objection. First, the crucial role of linguistic intentions for an adequate characterization of failures to make sense (Sections 3.8 and 4.2). Secondly, the distinction between actual and established meaning (Section 3.3). Each of these features gives rise to a specific version of the aforementioned objection. I will discuss them in turn.

4.4.1 A Theory of Sense Applied to Linguistic Intentions?

On the view I ascribed to Wittgenstein, a failure to make sense has to be characterized in terms of the speaker's linguistic intentions. I argued, for example, that for the *Tractatus* "A is an object" expresses a failure to make sense only relative to what the speakers wants to do with its component parts. Specifically, the sentence expresses the particular failure that the *Tractatus* is concerned to expose only if the speaker wants to use "object" to express a formal concept while also wanting to use it to apply a genuine concept to what is picked out by "A" (Sections 4.1). It may seem, therefore, that there is room for a theory of sense that determines whether a sentence makes sense or

---

[68] The crucial role of a distinctive form of the "we" in Wittgenstein's philosophy is one of the legacies of the work of Stanley Cavell (see especially Cavell 2015, chaps. 1 and 2). For an insightful discussion and elaboration, see Haase (2012).

[69] I am grateful to two anonymous referees for pressing this objection.

not on the basis of the linguistic intentions with which its parts are uttered and combined.

There is a question about how to construe the idea of "a sentence that is nonsensical in virtue of the linguistic intentions with which its parts are uttered and combined." On one construal, the idea is that, *when each intention is fulfilled*, the result is nonsense. This is easily dismissed by the view I ascribed to the *Tractatus*. Given the contextualism inherent in that view, linguistic intentions are always intentions to use words *to make sense*. Therefore, linguistic intentions cannot be fulfilled unless their fulfillment results in making sense. There is no such thing as a nonsensical *fulfillment* of a combination of linguistic intentions.

But there is also a way of construing the idea of "a sentence that is nonsensical in virtue of the linguistic intentions with which its parts are uttered and combined" that concedes the point just made. The claim would be that some combinations of linguistic intentions *cannot be jointly fulfilled*. A theory of sense applied to linguistic intentions would then specify conditions that combinations of such intentions must satisfy in order to be jointly fulfillable. When the conditions are not satisfied, *none* of the considered intentions is fulfilled. In particular, if the sentence makes no sense, no intention to use its component words as subsentential semantic units is fulfilled, in agreement with the version of the austere conception of nonsense I ascribed to the *Tractatus* (Section 3.7).

Notice that, in order to satisfy my definition of a theory of sense (Section 2.1), the view must provide a nonsensicality test whose input can be specified independently of its results. The view lays down conditions that a combination of subsentential linguistic intentions must meet in order to be jointly fulfillable. Hence, it must hold that it is possible to specify those intentions without already determining whether they are jointly fulfillable.

But I submit that this is not possible. If words can have subsentential meanings in some mutual combinations but not others, this is *already given* with the specification of the intentions to use the words with those meanings. This follows from the general principle that if something is already given with the specification of Φ-ing, it is already given also with the specification of the *intention to Φ*. Thus, once we have determined the speaker's subsentential linguistic intentions, we have already determined whether or not they are jointly fulfillable. For instance, determining that a speaker intends to use "object" to express a formal property already involves determining that there is no such thing as fulfilling that intention while also fulfilling the intention to use the word to express a genuine property. This is not an extra piece of information deliverable by a theory of sense.

It does not follow that, on the view I ascribed to the *Tractatus*, philosophical clarification cannot engage with linguistic intentions. On the contrary, it is essentially a work on what we intend to do with our words. But it is not the sort of work described by the objection under consideration. It is not a work that take place *after* the speaker's linguistic intentions have been determined, as the objection has it, but consists instead in clarifying *what* those intentions are. For Wittgenstein, failures to make sense consist precisely in the fact that we have a blurred perception of what we want to do with our words. Once the blur is overcome, there is nothing else that can or need to be done in order to dissolve the relevant illusion of sense. Recognizing that we wanted to use signs in ways that we can now see to be mutually exclusive *just is* to recognize that there wasn't anything determinate that we wanted to do with those signs – and thus, that our impression of making sense was only an illusion.

4.4.2 A Theory of Sense Applied to Established Meanings?

I suggested above that the Tractarian understanding of the Context Principle can be clarified by distinguishing actual and established meaning (Section 3.3). The established meaning of a sign is the potentiality, determined by the standing conventions of the language, to have a certain actual meaning. In the case of established subsentential meaning, it is the potentiality to make a certain con- tribution to the expression of a sentential content. For the *Tractatus*, I maintained, the parts of a nonsensical sentence do not have any actual meaning but may have established meanings. This can invite the objection that the view I ascribed to the *Tractatus* leaves room for a theory of sense operating at the level of established meaning: a theory that determines whether a sentence has or lacks established sense on the basis of the established meanings of its parts and the established significance of their mode of combination. Such a theory might determine, for instance, that given certain established meanings of "Socrates" and "is" and "an object," and the established significance of their concatenation, the sentence "Socrates is an object" has, relative to those established meanings, no established sense. My response runs parallel to the one I gave in the previous section to the objection from linguistic intentions. This is no accident, since actual meaning enters the specification of both linguistic intentions and estab- lished meaning.

First of all, there is a question about how to construe the idea of "a combin- ation of signs with established subsentential meanings that has no established sense." On one construal, the combination lacks established sense because, *when the semantic potentialities of its components and manner of combination are jointly actualized*, the result does not actually make sense. This is easily dismissed by the view I ascribed to the *Tractatus*. On that view, there is no such thing as an actualization of a subsentential semantic potentiality that leads to nonsense. Given the contextualism inscribed in that view, linguistic conventions are always conventions about how to use signs *to make sense*. Thus, if one succeeds in using a word in accordance with the conventions that constitute some established subsentential meaning, one also succeeds in using it to make sense.

However, one can construe the idea of "a combination of signs with established subsentential meanings that has no established sense" in a manner that grants the point just made. The idea would be that some combinations of established meanings *cannot be jointly actualized*. A theory of established sense applied to subsentential established meanings would specify conditions that combinations of such meanings must satisfy in order to be jointly actualizable. When the conditions are not satisfied, *none* of the subsentential potentialities taken into consideration is actualized. Such a view rules out the possibility of nonsensical sentences composed of actually meaningful parts and complies in the respect with the version of the austere conception of nonsense I ascribed to the *Tractatus*.

A theory of sense, as I defined it (Sections 2.1), operates at the level of actual meaning: its goal is to identify actual failures to make sense. The theory of established sense now under discussion is different, because its goal is to identify sentences that, relative to the standing conventions of the language, lack the potentiality to make sense. In order to be significantly analogous to the sort of theory of sense that I have been discussing, the theory must provide a test whose input can be specified independently of its results. The theory lays out conditions that combinations of signs with established meanings must satisfy in order to be jointly actualizable. Thus, it must hold that it is possible to specify the established subsentential meaning of a sign without already determining whether it is jointly actualizable with the established meanings of other signs.

I submit, in response, that this cannot be done. Established meaning is a potentiality. If what it is a potentiality *of* can subsist only in some combinations and not others, then this is already given with the specification of the potentiality. This follows from the general principle that if something is already given with the specification of X, it is already given also with the specification of the *potentiality to be X*. If there is no such thing as actually using the word "object" to express a formal concept while also using it to ascribe a genuine property, then this is given as soon as we specify the potentiality of the word "object" to express a formal concept. It is not an extra piece of information deliverable by a theory of established sense.

It does not follow that philosophical clarification, on the conception I ascribed to Wittgenstein, does not engage with established meanings. For Wittgenstein, I have argued, the illusions of sense that philosophy seeks to dispel derive from misleading patterns inscribed in our common language (Sections 1.2, 4.3). An investigation of established ways of using words, and established patterns of extending and modifying their standing meanings, is therefore essential to the activity of philosophical clarification. But the critical bite of this activity – i.e., its power to unmask illusions of sense – does not come from something that can be discovered *after* established ways of using words have been laid out. On the contrary, it lies entirely in this laying out. Illusions of sense arise because we are unclear about what is involved in certain established ways of using words. We don't fully know what we are doing when we are using words in those ways. Once these unclarities have been overcome, there is nothing else that can or need to be done in order to dispel illusions of sense.[70]

4.5 Conclusion

The distinction between sense and nonsense is essential to Wittgenstein's conception of philosophy and to his understanding of logical syntax (in the early work) and grammar (in the later work). Philosophy is a critical activity which aims to expose illusions of sense, and it does so by clarifying the logical syntax or grammar of linguistic expressions. There is a question, however, about how to construe this critical activity. I drew a contrast between a conception of philosophical critique that relies on a theory of sense, and one that does not. A theory of sense, as I defined it, aims to provide a nonsensicality test whose input can be specified independently of the results, and assumes that our linguistic capacity can be factorized into subcapacities whose successful exercise does not presuppose the successful exercise of the whole capacity. I used that contrast to schematize the exegetical debate about the nature and presuppositions of Wittgenstein's charges of nonsensicality. This yielded an account of what has been at stake in the dispute between resolute readers and some of their opponents over Wittgenstein's endorsement of an "austere"

---

[70] A possible objection, at this point, is that the contrast I have sought to draw (between conceptions of clarification that presuppose a theory of sense and conceptions that do not) is indeed in good standing, but irrelevant to the exegetical debate, because no significant commentator attributes to Wittgenstein the sort of "theory of sense" and "factorizing conception of language" that I have described. For a discussion pointing in this direction, see Shieh (2015). In Section 2, I argued that a number of prominent commentators – namely, Anscombe, Pears, Glock, and Hacker – do indeed ascribe to Wittgenstein a theory of sense. Even if the textual evidence I provided turned out to be unconvincing, the contrast I have drawn could still be useful for promoting the mutual understanding of resolute readers and their opponents by clarifying what resolute readers have taken to be at stake in the dispute over Wittgenstein's conception of nonsense and philosophical critique.

conception of nonsense. By focusing on the conception of language of the *Tractatus*, I argued that Wittgenstein subscribed to a strong version of the austere conception of nonsense. But I also tried to do justice to some of the objections commonly levelled against the austere conception of nonsense by introducing three improvements on previous presentations of the view:

i) I emphasized the importance of construing the sort of nonsense that philosophical clarification seeks to identify as a *failure* to make sense – and thus, as a case in which one does not make sense, but nonetheless *tries* to make sense and *takes oneself* to make sense. Not all cases of not making sense are of this sort, and this difference can be obscured by the insistence, characteristic of some resolute readers, that there is "logically only one kind of nonsense."

ii) I argued that failures to make sense cannot be characterized without reference to *linguistic intentions*, whose role cannot be vindicated from within the framework of the Frege-inspired dichotomy between logic and psychology adopted by some resolute readers.

iii) I introduced a distinction between *actual* and *established meaning* that goes beyond the existing proposals of resolute readers and I used it for three related purposes: to specify the proper scope of the Context Principle; to clarify the import of the austere conception of nonsense; and to account for linguistic productivity.

The fundamental insight of the austere conception of nonsense that I tried to develop and radicalize in this Element is its opposition to factorizing conceptions of language. Our linguistic capacity is unified in such a manner that a failure to make sense affects *all* aspects of the linguistic performance. When we fail to make sense, we do not *succeed* in exercising any subsidiary linguistic capacity that could provide the material to be tested for nonsensicality by a theory of sense.

References

Works by Wittgenstein

BB   *Preliminary Studies for the "Philosophical Investigations." Generally Known as The Blue and Brown Books.* 2nd ed. Oxford: Blackwell, 1969.

BT   *The Big Typescript: TS 213.* Edited by G. Luckhardt and M. Aue. Oxford: Blackwell, 2005. (References in the text give the page number of this edition, followed by the page number of the original typescript.)

LE   A Lecture on Ethics. *The Philosophical Review*, **74**(1) (1965), 3–12.

LO   *Letters to Ogden.* Edited by G. H. von Wright. Oxford: Blackwell, 1973.

LWL   *Wittgenstein's Lectures: Cambridge, 1930–1932.* Edited by D. Lee. Oxford: Blackwell, 1980.

MWL   *Wittgenstein's Lectures, Cambridge 1930–1933. From the Notes of G. E. Moore.* Edited by D. Stern, B. Rogers, and G. Citron. Cambridge: Cambridge University Press, 2016.

NB   *Notebooks 1914–1916.* Edited by G. H. von Wright and G. E. M. Anscombe. 2nd ed. Oxford: Blackwell, 1979.

NL   *Notes on Logic.* In M. Potter, *Wittgenstein's Notes on Logic*, pp. 276–289. Oxford: Oxford University Press, 2008.

PI   *Philosophical Investigations.* Translated by G. E. M. Anscombe. 2nd ed. Oxford: Blackwell, 1958.

PR   *Philosophical Remarks.* Edited by R. Rhees. Oxford: Blackwell, 1975.

RLF   Some Remarks on Logical Form. *Proceedings of the Aristotelian Society, Supplementary Volumes*, **9** (1929), 162–171.

TLP   *Tractatus Logico-Philosophicus.* Translated by C. K. Ogden and F. Ramsey. London: Kegan Paul, 1933. (In the quotations given in the text, this translation is occasionally modified.)

WVC   *Ludwig Wittgenstein and the Vienna Circle: Conversations Recorded by Friedrich Waismann.* Edited by B. F. McGuinness. Oxford: Blackwell, 1979.

Other Works

Anscombe, G. E. M. (1963). *An Introduction to Wittgenstein's Tractatus.* London: Hutchinson's University Library.

Baker, G. P. and Hacker, P. M. S. (2005). *Wittgenstein: Understanding and Meaning. Part I: Essays.* Vol. I of *An Analytical Commentary on the*

Philosophical Investigations. 2nd ed., extensively revised by P. M. S. Hacker. Oxford: Wiley-Blackwell.

Baker, G. P. and Hacker, P. M. S. (2009). *Rules, Grammar, and Necessity*. Vol. II of *An Analytical Commentary on the Philosophical Investigations*. 2nd ed., extensively revised by P. M. S. Hacker. Oxford: Wiley-Blackwell.

Bromberger, S. and Halle, M. (1986). On the Relationship of Phonology and Phonetics. In J. S. Perkell and D. H. Klatt, eds., *Invariance and Variability in Speech Process*, pp. 493–510. Hillsdale, NJ: Lawrence Erlbaum.

Bronzo, S. (2011). Context, Compositionality, and Nonsense in Wittgenstein's *Tractatus*. In R. Read and M. Lavery, eds., *Beyond the Tractatus Wars: The New Wittgenstein Debate*, pp. 84–111. Abingdon: Routledge.

Bronzo, S. (2012). The Resolute Reading and Its Critics: An Introduction to the Literature. *Wittgenstein-Studien*, **3**, 45–80.

Bronzo, S. (2017). Wittgenstein, Theories of Meaning, and Linguistic Disjunctivism. *European Journal of Philosophy*, **25**(4), 1340–1363.

Bronzo, S. (2019). Truth-bearers in Frege and the *Tractatus*. *Analiza i Egzystencja* **47**, 31–53.

Bronzo, S. and J. Conant (2017). Resolute Readings of the *Tractatus*. In H.-J. Glock and J. Hyman, eds., *A Companion to Wittgenstein*, pp. 175–194. Oxford: Blackwell.

Cavell, S. (1999). *The Claim of Reason: Wittgenstein, Skepticism, Morality, and Tragedy*. 2nd ed. Oxford: Oxford University Press.

Cavell, S. (2015). *Must We Mean What We Say?* Cambridge: Cambridge University Press.

Conant, J. (2000). Elucidation and Nonsense in Frege and Wittgenstein. In A. Crary and R. Read, eds., *The New Wittgenstein*, pp. 174–217. Abingdon: Routledge.

Conant, J. (2001). Two Conceptions of *Die Überwindung der Metaphysik*. In T. G. McCarthy and S. C. Stidd, eds., *Wittgenstein in America*, pp. 13–61. Oxford: Oxford University Press.

Conant, J. (2002). The Method of the *Tractatus*. In E. G. Reck, ed., *From Frege to Wittgenstein. Perspectives on Early Analytic Philosophy*, pp. 374–462. Oxford: Oxford University Press.

Conant, J. (2020a). Replies. In S. Miguens, ed., *The Logical Alien: Conant and His Critics*, pp. 321–1028. Cambridge, MA: Harvard University Press.

Conant, J. (2020b). Wittgenstein's Critique of the Additive Conception of Language. *Nordic Wittgenstein Review*, **9**, 7–36.

Conant, J. and C. Diamond (2004). On Reading the *Tractatus* Resolutely: Reply to Meredith Williams and Peter Sullivan. In M. Kölbel and B. Weiss, eds., *Wittgenstein's Lasting Significance*, pp. 44–99. Abingdon: Routledge.

Diamond, C. (1991). *The Realistic Spirit: Wittgenstein, Philosophy, and the Mind*. Cambridge, MA: MIT Press.

Diamond, C. (2000). Ethics, Imagination, and the Method of the *Tractatus*. In A. Crary and R. Read, eds., *The New Wittgenstein*, pp. 149–173. Abingdon: Routledge.

Diamond, C. (2005). Logical Syntax in Wittgenstein's *Tractatus*. *The Philosophical Quarterly*, **55**(218), 78–89.

Diamond, C. (2006). Peter Winch on the *Tractatus* and the Unity of Wittgenstein's Philosophy. In A. Pichler and S. Säätelä, eds., *Wittgenstein: The Philosopher and his Works*, pp. 141–170. Frankfurt: Ontos Verlag.

Diamond, C. (2011). The *Tractatus* and the Limits of Sense. In O. Kuusela and M. McGinn, eds., *The Oxford Handbook of Wittgenstein*, pp. 240–276. Oxford: Oxford University Press.

Diamond, C. (2019). *Reading Wittgenstein with Anscombe, Going on to Ethics*. Cambridge, MA: Harvard University Press.

Dobler, T. (2013). What Is Wrong with Hacker's Wittgenstein? On Grammar, Context, and Sense-Determination. *Philosophical Investigations*, **36**(3): 231–250.

Engelmann, J. M. (2011). What Wittgenstein's "Grammar" Is Not (On Garver, Baker and Hacker, and Hacker on Wittgenstein on "Grammar"). *Wittgenstein-Studien*, **2**, 71–102.

Frege, G. (1980). *The Foundations of Arithmetic*. 2nd ed. Evanston, IL: Northwestern University Press.

Glock, H.-J. (1996). *A Wittgenstein Dictionary*. Oxford: Blackwell.

Glock, H.-J. (2004). All Kinds of Nonsense. In E. Ammereller and E. Fisher, eds., *Wittgenstein at Work: Method in the Philosophical Investigations*, pp. 221–245. AbingdonLondon: Routledge.

Glock, H.-J. (2015). Nonsense Made Intelligible. *Erkenntnis*, **80**, 111–136.

Goldfarb, W. (1997). Metaphysics and Nonsense: On Cora Diamond's *The Realistic Spirit*. *Journal of Philosophical Research*, **22**, 57–73.

Gustafsson, M. (2020). Wittgenstein on Using Language and Playing Chess: The Breakdown of an Analogy and Its Consequences. In S. Miguens, ed., *The Logical Alien: Conant and His Critics*, pp. 202–221. Cambridge, MA: Harvard University Press.

Haase, M. (2012). Three Forms of the First Person Plural. In J. Conant and G. Abel, eds., *Rethinking Epistemology*, Vol. 2, pp. 229–256. Berlin: De Gruyter.

Hacker, P. M. S. (1986). *Insight and Illusion. Themes in the Philosophy of Wittgenstein*. 2nd ed. Oxford: Oxford University Press.

Hacker, P. M. S. (2000a). *Wittgenstein Mind and Will, Part I, Essays*. Vol. IV of *An Analytical Commentary on the Philosophical Investigations*. Oxford: Wiley-Blackwell.

Hacker, P. M. S. (2000b). Was He Trying to Whistle It? In A. Crary and R. Read, *The New Wittgenstein*, pp. 353–388. Abingdon: Routledge.

Hacker, P. M. S. (2001). Naming, Thinking and Meaning in the *Tractatus*. In P. M. S. Hacker, *Wittgenstein: Connections and Controversies*, pp. 170–190. Oxford: Oxford University Press.

Hacker, P. M. S. (2003). Wittgenstein, Carnap, and the New American Wittgensteinians. *The Philosophical Quarterly*, **53**(210), 1–23.

Hacker, P. M. S. (2013). What Is Wrong Indeed? *Philosophical Investigations*, **36**(3): 251–268.

Hacker, P. M. S. (2017). Metaphysics: From Ineffability to Normativity. In H.-J. Glock and J. Hyman, eds., *A Companion to Wittgenstein*, pp. 209–227. Oxford: Blackwell.

Hylton, P. (1990). *Russell, Idealism and the Emergence of Analytic Philosophy*. Oxford: Oxford University Press.

Jakobson, R. (1978). *Six Lectures on Sound and Meaning*. Cambridge, MA: MIT Press.

Johnston, C. (2007). Symbols in Wittgenstein's *Tractatus*. *European Journal of Philosophy*, **15**(3), 367–394.

Kern, A. (2017). *Sources of Knowledge. On the Concept of a Rational Capacity for Knowledge*. Cambridge, MA: Harvard University Press.

Kimhi, I. (2018). *Thinking and Being*. Cambridge, MA: Harvard University Press.

Kremer, M. (2002). Mathematics and Meaning in the *Tractatus*. *Philosophical Investigations*, **25**(3), 272–303.

McDowell, J. (1998). Criteria, Defeasibility, and Knowledge. In J. McDowell, *Meaning, Knowledge and Reality*, pp. 369–394. Cambridge, MA: Harvard University Press.

McDowell, J. (2010). Tyler Burge on Disjunctivism. *Philosophical Explorations*, **13**(3), 243–255.

McDowell, J. (2011). *Perception as a Capacity for Knowledge*. Milwaukee: Marquette University Press.

McDowell, J. (2013). Tyler Burge on Disjunctivism (II). *Philosophical Explorations*, **16**(3), 259–279.

McGinn, M. (2006). *Elucidating the Tractatus: Wittgenstein's Early Philosophy of Language and Logic*. Oxford: Oxford University Press.

Moore, A. W. (2003). Ineffability and Nonsense. *Proceedings of the Aristotelian Society, Supplementary Volumes*, **77**, 169–193.

Morris, M. (2008). *Wittgenstein and the Tractatus Logico-Philosophicus.* Abingdon: Routledge.

Moyal-Sharrock, D. (2007). The Good Sense of Nonsense. *Philosophia*, **82**, 147–177.

Nunez, T. (2019). Logical Mistakes, Logical Aliens, and the Laws of Kant's Pure General Logic. *Mind*, **128**(512), 1149–1180.

Pears, D. (1987). *The False Prison: A Study of the Development of Wittgenstein's Philosophy*, Vol. 1. Oxford: Oxford University Press.

Pears, D. (2007). *Paradox and Platitude in Wittgenstein's Philosophy.* Oxford: Oxford University Press.

Rödl, S. (2010). The Self-Conscious Power of Sensory Knowledge. *Grazer Philosophische Studien*, **81**, 135–151.

Shieh, S. (2015). How Rare is Chairman Mao? Dummett, Frege, and the Austere Conception of Nonsense. In B. Weiss, ed., *Dummett on Analytical Philosophy*, pp. 84–121. Basingstoke: Palgrave Macmillan.

Schönbaumsfeld, G. (2007). *A Confusion of the Spheres. Kierkegaard and Wittgenstein on Philosophy and Religion.* Oxford: Oxford University Press.

Schroeder, S. (2017). Grammar and Grammatical Statements. In H.-J. Glock and J. Hyman, eds., *A Companion to Wittgenstein*, pp. 252–268. Oxford: Blackwell.

Sullivan, P. (2003). Ineffability and Nonsense. *Proceedings of the Aristotelian Society, Supplementary Volumes*, **77**, 195–223.

Vanrie, W. (2017). *Logical Syntax and Nonsense in Wittgenstein's Tractatus.* BPhil Dissertation, University of Oxford.

Williams, M. (2004). Nonsense and Cosmic Exile: The Austere Reading of the *Tractatus*. In M. Kölbel and B. Weiss, eds., *Wittgenstein's Lasting Significance*, pp. 6–31. Abingdon: Routledge.

Cambridge Elements ≡

The Philosophy of Ludwig Wittgenstein

David G. Stern

University of Iowa

David G. Stern is a Professor of Philosophy and a Collegiate Fellow in the College of Liberal Arts and Sciences at the University of Iowa. His research interests include history of analytic philosophy, philosophy of language, philosophy of mind, and philosophy of science. He is the author of *Wittgenstein's Philosophical Investigations: An Introduction* (Cambridge University Press, 2004) and *Wittgenstein on Mind and Language* (Oxford University Press, 1995), as well as more than 50 journal articles and book chapters. He is the editor of *Wittgenstein in the 1930s: Between the 'Tractatus' and the 'Investigations'* (Cambridge University Press, 2018) and is also a co-editor of the *Cambridge Companion to Wittgenstein* (Cambridge University Press, 2nd edition, 2018), *Wittgenstein: Lectures, Cambridge 1930–1933, from the Notes of G. E. Moore* (Cambridge University Press, 2016) and *Wittgenstein Reads Weininger* (Cambridge University Press, 2004).

About the Series

This series provides concise and structured introductions to all the central topics in the philosophy of Ludwig Wittgenstein. The Elements are written by distinguished senior scholars and bright junior scholars with relevant expertise, producing balanced and comprehensive coverage of the full range of Wittgenstein's thought.

Cambridge Elements ≡

The Philosophy of Ludwig Wittgenstein

Elements in the Series

A full series listing is available at: www.cambridge.org/EPLW

Printed in the United States
by Baker & Taylor Publisher Services